GW00985993

Humans and AI

Humans and AI

The Future of Work

Jayne Mather

BEP
BUSINESS EXPERT PRESS
Leader in applied, concise business books

Humans and AI: The Future of Work

Copyright © Business Expert Press, LLC, 2025

Cover design by Charlene Kronstedt

Interior design by Exeter Premedia Services Private Ltd., Chennai, India

All rights reserved. No part of this publication may be reproduced, stored in a retrieval system, or transmitted in any form or by any means—electronic, mechanical, photocopy, recording, or any other except for brief quotations, not to exceed 400 words, without the prior permission of the publisher.

First published in 2025 by
Business Expert Press, LLC
222 East 46th Street, New York, NY 10017
www.businessexpertpress.com

ISBN-13: 978-1-63742-774-3 (paperback)
ISBN-13: 978-1-63742-775-0 (e-book)

Business Expert Press Service Collaborative Intelligence Collection

First edition: 2025

10 9 8 7 6 5 4 3 2 1

EU SAFETY REPRESENTATIVE
Mare Nostrum Group B.V.
Mauritskade 21D
1091 GC Amsterdam
The Netherlands
gpsr@mare-nostrum.co.uk

Description

Unlock the Future of Work: A Blueprint for Transformation

Step boldly into the new era of organizational excellence with this essential guide that navigates the intricacies of transformation powered by artificial intelligence (AI).

Elevate your leadership and strategy with insights into organizational design, process re-engineering, and cultivating an AI-centric mindset. This book offers executives and leaders a refined roadmap to radical redesign using advanced cognitive technologies.

- Embrace the imperative for change and the vital role of AI and intelligent automation in modern enterprises.
- Visualize the fully realized hyper-automation organization and aspire toward strategic goals that will place you at the forefront of progress.
- Master vital skills in process re-engineering, redefine essential roles, and attract the talent necessary to thrive in the age of AI.
- Gain insights into shifting mindsets and demonstrating visionary leadership through AI-driven decision making.
- Discover how the organizations of the future can make the world a better place by fully embracing emerging technology and the potential of your people.

Packed with actionable recommendations and enriched by real-world case studies, this guide presents a forward-thinking approach to future-proofing your organization.

Description

Contents

Testimonials

"As the author states, 'nothing changes unless you make changes'. In this era of AI-everything, change is imperative, but the only way to successfully do so is to understand (and use) the technologies and mindsets defining the future or work. This book is your guide. It accomplishes being a roadmap of the future, and a reference guide to the tools that will get you there. It does so while also painting a human-centric vision of work that is thoughtfully designed for the worker of the future. Read it. Use it. Succeed thanks to it."—**Ian Barkin, Founder, 2B Ventures and Author of *All Hands on Tech: The AI Powered Citizen Revolution***

"Humans and AI: The Future of Work *is a masterful synthesis of historical insights and cutting-edge strategies, essential for any leader aiming to harness the transformative power of artificial intelligence. This book deftly guides CEOs, CTOs, CAIOs, and Business Process Owners through the practical steps necessary to propel their organizations to the forefront of innovation, contention, and efficiency. It is not just a book but a comprehensive blueprint that marries sustainability with operational excellence, making it a cornerstone for organizations. A must-read before embarking on your AI journey, it sets a new standard for learning and transformation across industries. Unlock the future of work and step boldly into a new era of organizational excellence with this indispensable guide."*—**Ann Rosenberg, Senior Sustainability & Responsible AI Advisor, former SAP, EY, and Co-Founder United Nations Sustainable Development Goals (SDGs) Ambition**

"In Humans and AI: The Future of Work *the author Jayne Mather takes the reader on a carefully crafted journey exploring what may lie ahead and how best to prepare for the coming changes. My favorite part was learning about the 'Hyperautomation Organization'. For those looking for fresh perspectives, I recommend this book for both its sweeping vision of the future and its actionable recommendations."*—**Jim Spohrer, Co-Founder and Board Member, the International Society of Service Innovation Professional (ISSIP.org)**

"An insightful guide for leaders, blending AI-driven transformation with a human-centric approach to shape a more ethical and productive future. Jayne Mather offers a deep and multifaceted exploration of one of today's most important topics." —**Jeremy Adamson, Author and Leader in AI strategy**

*"*Humans and AI *is an incredibly comprehensive and practical guide for how AI is transforming the workplace and nature of work. It's the perfect companion to help business leaders understand and accelerate the disruptive power of AI. AI is optimising supply-chains, but it is also reinventing how we make traditional backoffice processes more effective. For organisations to survive and thrive in the age of AI they must unlock the innovative capacity of their workforce, enabling them to adapt to a rapidly changing world."* —**Daniel Hulme, CEO @ Satalia, Chief AI Officer @ WPP**

"If you think AI is just about robots taking jobs, think again. Humans and AI: The Future of Work *flips the narrative, proving AI can help businesses succeed while making work better for everyone. As someone passionate about emotional intelligence in AI, I found this book both timely and essential. The author shows that the real power of AI lies in its ability to elevate human potential—not replace it. This book is a call to action for leaders to redesign work in a way that benefits everyone."*—**Kendal Parmar, CEO & Co-Founder of Untapped AI**

"What happens when AI increasingly displaces demand for human labor while continuing to grow productivity to new heights? In this practical guide and insightful roadmap to navigating an AI-powered future, Jayne Mather highlights crucial technological dividends like Universal Basic Income and shorter workweeks among other smart changes. Discover how UBI can secure everyone's well-being while we redesign work to prioritize human fulfillment in a world of abundant technology."—**Scott Santens, Founder and CEO of Income To Support All Foundation**

"As the convergence of technological globalization advances, Human and AI: The Future of Work *must be an essential book to establish fundamental*

organizational structures that ensure business excellence, effective management and ethical governance for the future."—**Dr. Janét Aizenstros, MSc.D, Ph.D., MBA, former Chairwoman & CEO of Ahava Digital Group**

"*In a world fixated on the implications of AI, it's easy to overlook the immense opportunities it offers for business transformation. Through my work with Winder.AI, I've seen organizations waste valuable resources on projects misaligned with their business goals. Thankfully,* Humans and AI: The Future of Work *bridges this gap, presenting AI in clear, accessible language that every leader will be familiar with. This book empowers leaders to align AI integration with their teams, offering a perfect balance of actionable strategies and an inspiring vision of what's possible.*"—**Dr. Phil Winder, CEO, Winder.AI**

Foreword

Professor Leslie Willcocks London School of Economics and Political Science

Dr. John Hindle, Managing Partner, Knowledge Capital Partners.

Robotic process automation takes the robot out of the human. It tries to say goodbye to, by automating, all those short cycles, mindless data, and information processing tasks. Intelligent automation and artificial intelligence (AI) build on computing, visual and natural language processing, memory, algorithm, and machine learning developments to attempt, amongst other things, to put the human into the robot. Digital transformation aims at a whole organizational change founded on emerging digital technologies. The difficulties rise exponentially across these endeavors. Why? Because, despite the massive rhetoric otherwise, no technology is a silver bullet divorced from its organizational and managerial contexts. We consistently find, over the decades of research, advisory, and practice, that with automation and digital technologies, 25 percent of the challenges relate to technology, and 75 percent are organizational and managerial.

It is a delight therefore to welcome a book that not only recognizes this reality but also details in a most engaging way the hard-won practices that really do deliver the holy grail of superior digital business value. At the heart of this has to be redesign and re-engineering. To be frank, every organization we encounter could do with a regular makeover. When you add in the desire to become digital, organizational readiness is very mixed, as, unsurprisingly, are the outcomes.

In the present climate, this is perfectly understandable. Organizations are heavily siloed. Have a look at your processes, structures, data, technology, skill sets, culture, strategy, and management. And digital dislikes siloes. Then there is the challenge of integrating digital with a plethora of legacy technologies. Organizational change is notoriously difficult, but how else are you going to leverage the massive business potential of these technologies as they come on-stream? Automation and digital require focus when there are so many more immediate, urgent, serious priorities. Automation and digital also take time. On the big picture, it has taken anything from 6 to 24 years for a major technology to be taken up by 90 percent of organizations in a developed economy. Digital transformation is a misnomer; it's much more a digital evolution. Digital also requires building distinctive core capabilities. In our research into over a thousand businesses, these are digital strategy, integrated planning, embedded culture, governance, change management, digital platform, and navigation. Typically in any sector, 20 percent of organizations have built these to the level where they outperform by two to six times all others on profitability, revenue, dividends, and market valuation. Without key actions by what we call in descending performance order the "follower," "laggard," and "struggler" enterprises, the gap will widen.

Time for the majority to catch up, and this book is an indispensable aid. It does not fall into the trap of advocating "best practice" replication of what leaders have done. Instead, starting from where you are, the author's preferred approach is to take you back to laying the foundations stone-by-stone, step-by-step.

For the author, purpose in the form of business imperatives drives everything. A view of the possible endpoint is a key motivator, and the first chapter provides a fascinating vision of the office in 20 years' time established on the criteria of comfort, connection, collaboration, and childcare. Yes, you want to be there. Chapter 2 provides a galvanizing overview to help the reader understand in detail the pragmatic process advocated. Unlike in all too many books, it's not a Yellow Brick Road, but it is tarmacked, highly usable, and gets you from A to B efficiently. A key message is that you will have to invest in the management, technical, and organizational skills to use the roadmap. Such investment is, we know, in the present climate a difficult call to make, but if cost is the paramount consideration, then as we know from researching the "laggards" and "strugglers" in all the major sectors, not making the investment decision is going to cost a lot more.

We do not need to take you through the ensuing chapters in detail. Suffice it to say that practitioners are in for a treat. So much salient, "on the nose" information, lessons, and practices delivered in a concise, very accessible, and engaged way. What amazed us was the level of practical, highly informed useable detail. It becomes clear that not only does the author really know what they are talking about, but they are also quietly brilliant at communicating it.

The book concludes with convincing arguments supporting the view that with informed management practices and some necessary guardrails, automation, and digital can and will form a constructive basis for future work and society. If people follow the prescriptions in this book, we too have no doubt there is a lot to be optimistic about. If you want a comprehensive, pragmatic, useable, highly informed, and intelligent guide to deploying automation and digital, you are about to start reading it.

Leslie Willcocks and John Hindle are authors of *Maximizing Value With Automation and Digital Transformation: A Realist's Guide* (Palgrave, 2024).

Acknowledgments

Thank you to Scott and Charlene at Business Expert Press, and to Kubra and the team at Kriyadocs, for believing in the value of the book and for all your help during the publishing process. Thank you to Leslie and John for writing such an insightful and supportive foreword. Thank you to all of the wonderful experts who wrote a testimonial. Your reviews and endorsements mean the world to me. It has been humbling and hugely validating to receive such positive reviews from thought leaders such as yourselves. I'm so pleased my writing has resonated with you and look forward to collaborating with you to realize a better world through advocating for the responsible use of this technology.

Personally, now, for my son Ethan, my fellow author, thank you for making me smile every day and remember me and you can do anything we set our minds to. My son Ethan wrote *The Mutated Man* at 10 years old and was offered his first publishing deal at 11. I had to wait till I was in my 40s, I'm sure this kid thinks this is normal and easy; but for those of you reading this, please do go find his book and support a young author. For Adrian, you've made it from my top five men to the second-best man in the world, still behind only to my Dad. Mum, Dad, and Stuart, please do continue to show off about the author in the family, your belief in me led me from a rebellious wild teenager to an amazing career and realizing my ambitions. Hugh and Francesca, my favorite niece and nephew have to get a mention, I can't wait to see how you put those amazing brains and positive attitudes to work. For the rest of my friends and family, you all got a call out in my last book and I have to say the muted response to my second book compared to my first is noted :) but seriously, I'm the luckiest woman in the world to have you all in my corner.

Thank you to the readers; I hope you picked up the book ready to transform your organization, and I would love to hear from you about your results and ideas. But I also hope you put the book down believing how this technology can benefit the world. If you share this vision, please do tell others about this book.

Full disclosure, as we have to be transparent about our use of AI. There were occasions I tried using it as a writing assistant to review my work, but I certainly couldn't 'foster' the generic suggestions. Generative AI has amazing potential but it doesn't yet compare to the unique voice, writing style, and experience of real experts. I did however, use it to generate some of the diagrams. See if you can tell which? I couldn't use it for all of them though, some of the images it produced were just awful and inaccurate. Thank goodness we don't want AI to completely take over, right? It's about using it where it makes sense to accelerate the productivity of humans. Read on, and I'll tell you more about why and how.

Who Is This Book for

This book provides value for **organizational leadership** and **tech enthusiasts**, including roles such as:

- Chief executive officer (CEO)
- Chief technology officer (CTO)
- Chief information officer (CIO)
- Chief operations officer (COO)
- Chief strategy officer (CSO)
- Chief human resources officer (CHRO)
- Chief finance officer (CFO)
- Chief AI officer (CAIO)
- Head of automation
- Head of digital transformation
- Head of organizational change and development
- People/HR directors
- Head of IT
- Business process owners
- Continuous improvement leads
- Business and process analysts
- Automation developers
- AI/machine learning engineers
- Data science analysts

Objectives

- Provide a clear roadmap for organizations looking to transition into AI-led automation-first models, emphasizing the importance of using change management, process re-engineering, and intelligent automation.
- Break down the complexities of cognitive technologies, offering accessible explanations and real-world use cases to empower readers to embrace and implement these ideas.
- Encourage leaders to think big, aligning short-term goals with long-term aspirations, emphasizing adaptability, sustainability, and a future-proof organizational design.
- Address potential pitfalls and challenges in the AI-first journey, drawing on lessons learned, case studies, and expert insights to ensure sustainable change and success.
- Emphasize the continued importance of people-centric values in the age of automation.

CHAPTER 1

The Imperative for Organizational Redesign

I'm pretty old school, not old, just I've seen some things.

I've seen typewriters be replaced by PCs and office software. I've seen mainframe systems move to ERP systems, I remember doing business before the internet and overseeing paper brochures and catalogs being replaced by e-commerce websites. I threw away the to-do lists when we got project planning software. I've seen data storage move from filing cabinets to physical servers and then to cloud virtualization, and with the cloud came sharing and collaboration tools, as well as many web-based niche systems. I've seen *big data* move from our reports and spreadsheets into data warehouses and dashboards for visualization and analytics (although I still love a good spreadsheet) and so digital transformation has always been part of my working life, even before that term was the buzzword we all use today.[1]

Many organizations have already implemented automation and the growing market here is huge; analysts predict the intelligent automation market will grow from $14b in 2023 to $29b in 2028.[2] Artificial intelligence (AI), though not new, has galvanized organizations of late to explore how large language models and generative AI can help them in their goals. The organizations that have and will succeed are those that have adapted to technological advances and are equipped to withstand the disruption these changes bring.

We are in the information age, the fourth industrial revolution, and this book is here to help you plan and prepare for the future. From radical redesigns to small steps, this book will help you know what you can do now, and where you need to end up.

The "future of work" is not just a phrase, it keeps us abreast of the trends and advances that will shape how we do things. The COVID-19 pandemic, for example, accelerated a trend toward remote working, this was often predicted, and it was possible way before the pandemic, but remote working went from a future of work concept, to being the way we all did the work. There is still some resistance of course (micromanagers and commercial estate owners I'm looking at you), and the future of the office is still subject to discussion, but those who wanted to continue operating through the pandemic, and continue driving performance through a positive employee experience afterward, moved with the trends and thrived. That is exactly what I want to equip you to do: the shift will be from predictions, to trends, to the way we do things. I want you with me on the way.

You'll have heard before of the infamous examples like Kodak, Blockbuster, Nokia, Toys"R"Us, and BlackBerry. These case studies remain as notes of caution to those organizations that fail to adapt to changes in the market and to the opportunities that technology brings.

We're all familiar now with seeing self-checkouts in the supermarkets, ordering from an app in a restaurant, or interacting with a chatbot instead of a customer services person. We know robotics have been used in the warehousing and manufacturing industries for some decades now. Their competitors now find it difficult not to join them, as they experience enhanced productivity, efficiency, and cost savings. You need to plan for your organization to utilize the latest technology, particularly AI and automation, so your competitors will find it difficult not to join you too.

The benefits will be your adaptability and robust resilience to the market, increased value realization, and speed in providing your service. Embracing a digital mindset drives further innovation in your people and in your IT landscape. Building an organization that is focused on utilizing AI and automation frees up your people to work on satisfying, value-added work that matters. By eliminating repetitive and manual work, this can give you a laser-sharp focus on delivering your business strategy and goals. Cost savings and increased revenue enable you to invest further in your people or in your future innovations or potential mergers and acquisitions.

This book will help you navigate the principles of organizational design and development and apply them to an organization that is powered by automation, AI, and cognitive computing. I will equip you with the knowledge and inspiration to re-engineer your processes with the future in mind and to understand how you can apply the tech throughout all your business functions. Simply put, this book will help you be the organization the future needs.

A Day at the Office

Indulge me for a moment, and let's take a jump through time and imagine what a day in the office could be like 10 to 20 years from now.

The future of work needs a new approach to organizational design. With a fusion of human ingenuity and AI, workplaces can become hubs of innovation, collaboration, and well-being. This book can help organizations adapt to the changing landscape, empower their employees, and harness the power of technology to drive productivity, efficiency, and growth.

I'm looking forward to visiting our office today, I usually work remotely so the opportunity to spend time with my colleagues from around the world is exciting for me. Our office recruits only the best of the best from a global talent pool, so it's likely to be a stimulating couple of days of strategizing and collaborating on our latest solution. Our profits have seen a huge increase since we redesigned our organization over a decade ago, so the travel costs are always approved as long as we continue to demonstrate the value of meeting up once a quarter.

My day begins with my commute to the office in my electric autonomous vehicle. I use the time to catch up on my reading, podcasts, and to interact with my personal coach who mentors me on my personal growth goals as well as on the strategy for my team in the years ahead. Learning and development is high on the agenda at my company, so I have access to the world's best coaches either virtually, holographically, or personally. Not to mention unlimited access to the leading training courses in my chosen expertise.

As I arrive, the gates to the secure facility open as it recognizes both my face and number plate and autonomously guides me to a parking space in my preferred area: well-lit but still giving me enough of a distance to enjoy a short, scenic walk to the reception.

The holographic receptionist warmly welcomes me and provides me with the key updates I need for the day. The overhead screen uses retinal projection that can only be viewed by myself and not bystanders, it can convey confidential information but today it just gives me an update of the times my colleagues are due to arrive as well as the location of the office space I have booked today.

As the first to arrive, I head to our space for the day and arrange the moveable furniture and walls the way we need them. I decide which walls will be used as screens, whiteboards and which just as walls, deciding against any sound-proof features for the day. The smart windows I leave as they are, as I enjoy our view and don't need any of the virtual scenes today. I choose a standard desk for the day, knowing some of my colleagues prefer the standing desks and exercise integrated desks available and as I take my seat, the smart desk uses my biometrics to automatically adjust to my preferences and ergonomic needs.

The office sensors adjust the lighting to my preference and thankfully they know I like to be warm so I can already feel the filtered, quality air warming around me as I contemplate my next task. The user interface prompts me to consider if I need any drinks or snacks, and I have the option of heading to the smart kitchen or having a robot or drone deliver to me. I choose my usual cup of tea and it arrives within the minute, strong but milky, and with Yorkshire tea, exactly how I like it.

I can use either my handheld or desktop device to check on our operations and team performance to ensure I'm as up-to-date as possible before I begin interacting with the team. I can see a seamless view of both my human and robot colleagues' performance. My robot colleagues deal with nearly all of our mundane, repetitive tasks as our people are worth so much more than spending their time on those. But the robots in our team (named after our favorite British rock stars) are capable and responsible for many complex tasks too, and it is these I pay close attention to as I analyze the changes and decisions they have made as they continue to self-learn. I am pleased with some of the recent success, and I choose to share the results with my wider company immediately so we can all celebrate the achievements, as well as enable other teams to take the learnings into their own projects.

Next, I check in with my personal AI assistant and see if there is anything I need to review. My assistant, I call him Keith as the gentlemanly voice I chose for him reminds me of my Grandad, has worked with me for a long time now and I trust him implicitly to reply to emails on my behalf and schedule or respond to meeting requests. There are still often new situations that arise where he knows I will want to review the response before he sends it, as well as contribute input of my own. This also helps to train him further as he understands my decisions, writing style, knowledge, experience, and behaviors each time we interact.

I am alerted that some of my team members are beginning to arrive now, and I head over to say hello knowing a few of them will have their cute children with them to take advantage of the state-of-the-art creche facilities on site. Although working from home enables me to be my best, most productive self the majority of the time, it makes me proud to know our office is designed to accommodate these needs.

A while back, when we realized we didn't need the office to be able to house everyone at the same time anymore, we redesigned our office around what we called the Four Cs:

Comfort: for our well-being and positive mental health, to prevent us feeling isolated at home we can choose to spend time in the office, or at a number of co-working spaces we have access to.

Connection: our team performs to its highest standards when we build trust and relationships together by connecting personally when we deem it necessary.

Collaboration: some projects and problems, strategies and ideas can benefit by having the brightest minds in the room with you.

Childcare: on-site childcare ensures everyone has the same opportunity to do meaningful work that gives them purpose.

It is nice to hear from the newest member of the team how much they appreciate the decor and lush greenery around the space, which, along with the renewable energy sources, is part of what makes the office sustainable and carbon neutral. He has just finished his site induction via virtual reality, but I still walk him around and introduce him to the team members and show off the office space here that we value so much.

As the remaining team members have arrived from their travels, with only a few of them choosing to join us both virtually and holographically, we begin our meetings for the day and spend a couple of hours presenting, and problem-solving and deciding which ideas to prioritize for the next quarter to improve our service, and innovations for our clients. With a global team we appreciate that automatic language translation is provided via our AI to enable the most inclusive communicative experience throughout, then as the meetings draw to a close transcripts and images of our notes are captured for recap should we need them.

My health wristband alerts me to my nutritional needs for the day and we debate whether to leave the office but decide the office restaurant menu for the day is too tempting, having been carefully curated knowing of our arrival. My wristband also alerts me to the need for movement too, I often have a run in the early afternoon but decide a walk would be better after our amazing lunch. Our office values the emotional and mental well-being of the team so I can opt to sync my wristband with the organization to monitor my mood, stress, overall health, and even provide advice, alerts, and assistance should any emergencies arise.

The rest of the afternoon we split to work on smaller project proposals, we test our ideas on the digital twin of our organization so we can carefully simulate the impact of any changes we make to our operations. As we brainstorm our latest project, I slip on my augmented reality (AR) headset, and the room transforms. 3D models of our product hover in the air, allowing us to manipulate and examine them from every angle. This immersive environment makes our discussions far more productive. We then analyze the results as a full team again, and by full team, this time I mean both the people in the team and Bowie the robot who is a specialist in predictive analytics and modeling, which aids our decisions and output. We're comfortable with the results and decide to inform our leadership of the progress we have made today.

Some of the leaders join us virtually for an hour and offer their insights. We love that our leadership fully trusts us to make the right decisions, as we trust them to provide the inspiration and visionary leadership we need. Leadership values are very much those of compassion, emotional intelligence, empathy, and driving high performance through people and skills development. Our organization may have been designed to be automation-first to give us the competitive edge we need to make a difference in the world, but our values are still people-centric. Because no matter what technology advances we use, it is motivated people that make things happen here.

At the end of the day, some of my team opt to return home to their families, some will socialize in the local area, and some will utilize the serviced apartments above the office space, designed especially for the colleagues and guests who will travel to visit us.

As the robot cleaners begin their rounds, I decide to stay late tonight to make the most of my time here and prepare for our team meeting again in the morning. I'll probably leave early in the afternoon tomorrow and enjoy my usual three-day weekend afforded to me by the organizations ability to turn productivity gains into a four-day working week with no loss of pay, returning refreshed and ready to put my all into a workplace that gives me a sense of achievement, purpose, and belonging.

CHAPTER 2

Designing the Intelligent Organization

To create an intelligent organization, I'm going to offer some specific recommendations in the book to design an organization where people, processes, systems, and robots work seamlessly together to deliver your business goals.

But first, let's start with understanding the principles of organizational design (OD), the questions we need to ask ourselves, and the decisions we may need to take. There is no *one-size-fits-all* so starting with this broad foundation will enable you to create a bespoke design aligned with your vision.

Let's look at a couple of definitions.

- 'Organisation design, or re-design, focuses on aligning the shape and structure of an organisation with its strategy'.[1]
- Organisations are contrived social systems that are created by like-minded groups of persons to pursue and hopefully achieve a stated goal; and this process of creation is known as organisational design.[2]

That helps us to know we need to start with strategy and goals.

If you're reading this book, then you're interested in transforming your work, so I want you to consider the principle that everything that can be automated, should be automated. But why? We need to start with the why.

When your organization has fully integrated artificial intelligence and automation into all your teams and processes, what does that help you achieve?

Is it for increased revenue? If so, why? What will that help you do? Is it so that revenue can drive further innovation in your products or R&D? Is it to reinvest in your people? Is it to deliver more value to your shareholders? Is it to generate more cash to acquire other companies for your portfolio, or to spend more on marketing and tactical strategies to increase your market share?

Another example may be to enhance employee experience. But why? Is it to free your people up to spend more time on client relationships? Is it to attract the top talent? Is it so your people can spend more time on continuous improvement or problem-solving? Is it to win awards or be classified as a "great place to work"? Is it to allow more time for innovation, creativity, and experimentation?

Is it to lower costs, improve efficiency, and reduce waste? Why? I could go on, there are so many benefits that we could, and will, discuss but there is no point in me telling you that your goals for redesigning your organization should be to pursue a strategy of automating everything that can be automated, you need to be able to articulate why this is important.

Implementing AI or automation, like any new technology, ways of working, or changes to people's roles, amounts to a significant organizational change. Which doesn't just happen without effort. The organization needs to be designed in such a way that can facilitate, enable, and sustain this change and that's why we need to start looking at the design of the organization to make the change a success and for us to be able to deliver on that ultimate why.

Factors to Consider for a Successful Organizational Redesign

Vision

The leadership will need to craft a vision for the future state of the organization to start off our design process. The vision statement should be a succinct, compelling statement outlining **why** your organization is undergoing a redesign to support the holistic integration of this technology. Your vision verbalizes the *bigger picture* and should resonate with every business function and provide clarity. Having a vision provides an aspirational direction for the organization, encourages change acceptance, and enables an innovative mindset to consider *the art of the possible* in what transformational value AI and automation can deliver.

More advice for writing your vision will be covered in Chapter 5.

Strategy

The strategy will define the approach to realize our vision. This will need to be provided over several layers: a big, bold strategy for the whole organization and then more detail as this is cascaded down to divisions, business functions, and potentially teams.

The strategy should include milestones and dates, but whereas the big and bold overarching vision can extend far into the future to give us direction, the detail of the **how** should only cover what you can commit to doing in the next one to two years. You will need to refresh and update this strategy regularly to reflect your current progress and to consider any changes as technology advances.

More advice for setting strategies will be covered in Chapter 5.

Assessment

Assessing the *as-is* state of the organization is key to making progress. This involves a detailed look at the entire ecosystem of your organization to understand what supports our vision and strategy, and where we may have gaps. Internally you will need to analyze your systems and infrastructure; your culture and values; your people, performance, and organizational structures; your processes and ways of working, data sources, challenges, weaknesses, and opportunities. It's important to assess externally too to understand how your vision is likely to perform in the market and against competitors.

More advice for assessing the organization will be covered in Chapter 6.

Leadership

Leadership will play a pivotal role in steering the organization toward an automation-centric design. Depending on the results of our assessment and gap analysis, this is likely to be the first place we focus, and executive coaching is strongly recommended. Desired leadership behaviors encompass driving an innovative and creative mindset, effectively articulating the benefits, providing coaching, and embracing boldness. Securing buy-in from this group to align to the vision will be imperative to drive the redesign.

More advice for desired leadership behaviors will be covered in Chapter 11.

Culture and Values

Culture and values will be the catalyst needed to make your redesign a success. The emphasis lies in cultivating a consistent culture that is not only professed but actively practiced and evident throughout the whole organization. This involves a thorough examination of the underlying principles influencing behaviors and how and why tasks are performed, with a focus on ensuring alignment with the vision.

Examine your values and assess whether they support the organization being progressive, ambitious, and based on trust. A culture of open communication, experimentation, and collaboration is essential to support your vision and redesign. Your assessment may indicate new culture and values are needed, this should be done in consultation with leadership and all staff, everyone needs to be heard and have a contribution to make it a collective coalition toward achieving your vision.

Chapter 10 will help you more in this space.

Roadmap

It's crucial to thoroughly outline a comprehensive timeline that charts the journey from the current state to the future state. Prioritize strategic milestones and success criteria, crafting a roadmap that achieves a balanced blend of a visually engaging version for effective communication to the organization, as well as a detailed iteration tailored to provide guidance at the functional level. Ensure this roadmap aligns with your vision and strategy and makes it clear how the contributions of each business function are important.

Leadership engagement is vital to communicate the roadmap's significance and to drive its integration into the organizational fabric. Additionally, consider involving key stakeholders in the roadmap development process to enhance collaboration and buy-in across departments.

I'll give you some more recommendations in Chapter 7.

Collaborative Workforce of Humans and AI

This is a huge one, there are some recommendations in this book I may delicately suggest, but this one, I might insist on you implementing.

Let's envision a collaborative environment where humans and robots seamlessly function within all teams, intricately integrated into every facet of the business. Line managers assume the responsibility for overseeing the day-to-day operations of both artificial and human employees, ensuring a harmonious and efficient amalgamation of skills and capabilities. AI and automation should not be an unseen back-office function led by IT, it should be present within every operational team with each process carefully redesigned to complement the strengths of both human and robot workers. Our redesign will be built on this core principle.

I'll cover this more throughout the book as it's important enough to say more than once.

Structure and Roles

Changes in the organizational structure and roles should be aligned with the overarching business strategy and culture, necessitating thoughtful HR consultation for seamless role transitions. This should be planned from the beginning, with decisions made on who you will need in each function, what roles they will do once automation is fully integrated, and how each team will be structured using a collaborative workforce.

Although decisions will need to be made up front, it is wise to avoid putting these changes into writing until your organization is aligned on the future vision and the changes required, and employees are actively involved in making the transition a success. If employees see organizational structures or job titles changing too early it could invoke anxiety about the change or their job security.

Role mapping will be required with a meticulous exploration of the organizational structure. It involves identifying new roles essential for delivering the benefits of cognitive computing, adjusting existing roles to meet the evolving demands of how the work will be carried out, and discerning roles that may no longer be required, such as data entry for example.

As an integral part of organizational redesign, this process also prompts a reconsideration of hierarchical structures. The shift toward more agile frameworks is recommended to accommodate the fluidity and flexibility demanded by hyperautomation and establish an environment conducive to innovation and rapid responsiveness to change.

Chapter 9 will provide more advice for this process.

Benefits and Value

Articulating the benefits of intelligent automation is a fundamental step in aligning the technology with the overall organizational strategy. Defining the advantages, whether they be increased efficiency, cost reduction, or innovation acceleration, provides a clear narrative for how cognitive computing aligns with and propels the organizational mission forward.

Agreeing on the focus for the benefits at the beginning of your redesign will keep you focused on what to use AI for and what to automate, and what information to track to prove benefits realization.

Chapters 3, 4, and 6 will provide more examples of the benefits and use cases for intelligent automation.

Organizational Change Management

Change management assumes a central role in enabling the organizational transition. Change management extends beyond just addressing surface-level change resistance and requires a whole new mindset necessary to ensure the seamless integration of a transformative redesign. Change management becomes the catalyst for cultivating a culture of adaptability and innovation. It involves a thorough examination of the current organizational state, identifying potential points of resistance, and proactively devising strategies to mitigate risk and promote acceptance and engagement.

The change management process is described further in Chapter 10.

Centre of Excellence (CoE)

The CoE will be a key function to consider in your OD. This team takes the lead in driving the implementation of the technology, championing its benefits, and advocating for widespread adoption. The team can be a mix of internal and external talent but to prove maximum impact at an early stage, technical prowess will be of critical importance.

The CoE is fundamental for orchestrating swift and effective deployment of automated solutions across multiple business functions. The CoE should strategically prioritize high-impact use cases, delivering quick wins that demonstrate tangible benefits and set the stage for broader, scalable integration.

Mentoring citizen developers should also be a key focus of the CoE, contributing to the development of internal talent and being able to scale automations across the organization faster. The CoE, along with a chief AI officer or head of automation role, empowers individuals to actively contribute to the initiative, ensuring a workforce that can rapidly adopt new processes to meet the goals of the project.

We'll get more advice on this topic in Chapter 7.

Talent Matrix

HR will need to help you review or implement a talent matrix to help support any OD. As well as identifying the technical skills required, a talent strategy is important for a workforce that is not only capable but also enthusiastic about meeting AI and tech-focused goals.

Equally vital is the formulation of a robust talent retention plan, recognizing that an engaged and motivated workforce is instrumental in achieving your goals. This plan encompasses measures to cultivate a work environment that values continuous learning, innovation, and adaptability. In doing so, the organization not only retains its top talent but also becomes an attractive hub for new talents aspiring to contribute to the future of work.

Lots more advice on talent to come in Chapter 9.

Initiatives and Projects

To realize the vision of seamless human and AI collaboration, it's essential to reassess the organization's entire approach to projects by leveraging established methodologies like PRINCE2, agile, or Six Sigma.

PRINCE2 could provide a framework for effective project management, ensuring that multiple, parallel initiatives align with organizational goals and are executed with precision. Agile methodology, known for its flexibility and responsiveness to change, becomes particularly relevant in the context of automation-first organizations. The dynamic nature of intelligent automation demands an iterative and adaptive project management approach, and building automation solutions iteratively is a great use of agile principles.

Simultaneously, Six Sigma brings its focus on process improvement and reduction of variability, aligning perfectly with our goals for redesign. By embedding lean thinking and Six Sigma principles into projects, organizations can enhance the efficiency and effectiveness of automation initiatives, ensuring that they not only meet but exceed expectations.

This strategic reconsideration of project management methodologies, and the digital skills these initiatives require, is not just about adopting industry best practices; it's about redefining the organizational DNA to embrace agility, innovation, and continuous improvement.

We'll look deeper when we re-evaluate our processes in Chapter 8.

Data and Insights

Data and insights are key enablers in organizational redesign, ensuring that every step toward becoming an intelligent organization is guided by insightful data. Data are a transformative necessity fueling decision making and process optimization.

By leveraging the potential of big data and predictive analytics, organizations can anticipate challenges, identify opportunities, and proactively formulate a roadmap for the deployment of AI and automation. Data transparency and visualization ensure that decision making is informed, and access to quality data enables agile and adaptive scaling across business functions.

Quality data are key enablers for organizational redesign and will come up again in Chapter 12.

Decision-Making Culture

We need a culture where decision making is not just a procedural step, or a need for endless meetings and approval cycles, but an autonomous and insights-led instinct. Organizations need to empower their teams to make quick but informed, data-driven decisions.

Drawing inspiration from industry exemplars like Amazon, organizations can learn valuable lessons in decision-making dynamics. The distinction between reversible and nonreversible decision making, as exemplified by Amazon, is an excellent guiding principle to emulate. Reversible decisions, delegated to lead roles, managers, and expert employees, allow for experimentation, speed, and flexibility, while nonreversible decisions should only made by leadership and should demonstrably support the strategy.[3]

By determining this approach in your redesign, you can ensure that each step in the automation journey is backed by thoughtful analysis with an emphasis on autonomous teams, which aligns with our recommendations for achieving the overarching strategy.

Skills and Development

Skills and development initiatives are integral to addressing the digital skills gap.

Using a coaching approach with leadership is crucial, ensuring a focus not of technical proficiency but instead of a mindset aligned with driving strategic goals and an emphasis on progressive innovation.

Employee training comes next, creating a workforce that not only possesses technical capabilities but also embraces the cultural shift brought by hyperautomation. Once role mapping is complete, we can identify employees who may need retraining to move into different roles, who may need upskilling to enable them to become citizen developers or part of the automation CoE, as well as providing employees with skills such as problem-solving, process improvement, or relationship building. Those employees who are freed up from the repetitive tasks they used to do will need to develop their skills to add value through human creativity and connection.

We'll cover skills development more in Chapter 9.

Governance and Risk

The redesign will necessitate an overhaul in the realm of policies, compliance, security, and ethics. This involves a comprehensive reassessment and potential redesign of existing organizational guidelines, particularly as your workforce will no longer consist of just people. However, this redesign should be focused on the advantages that intelligent automation can bring as robot workers can add a high level of robustness and resilience to your compliance and security procedures.

A comprehensive risk management strategy is required to delve into the risk around resource, timelines, impact on operations or customers, alignment with regulatory, legal, or compliance aspects in order to mitigate any potential pitfalls.

Equally significant is an evaluation of the risks associated with maintaining the status quo. A candid exploration of the consequences of resisting change is essential and will contribute to influencing and engaging with key stakeholders. This involves an introspective analysis of how the organization might lag behind in the market and the potential threats it could face by not embracing the transformative potential of emerging technologies.

Chapter 13 will give us more of a guide into governance and risk.

Ownership and Accountability

Who should own the agenda for organizational redesign?

- Leadership should own the overall strategy and drive progress.
- HR is instrumental in identifying the right structure and developing a comprehensive talent retention plan. Their focus should be on crafting an employee experience meticulously tailored to align with the aspirations of the automation-first approach.
- Learning and development will be pivotal in initiating programs of skills development and coaching.
- Change management teams will strategically address not only resistance but also own the change plan influencing the human side of the transformation, emphasizing effective communication and stakeholder engagement.
- IT should lead the selection of the right tools but also the construction of a robust infrastructure capable of supporting the scale and speed required.
- Operations will be responsible for the implementation of AI and automation into their day-to-day operations as well as focusing on minimal disruption during the transition.
- Additionally, you should consider a governance council that includes leads from all of the above areas as well as representation from finance to support budget and resource allocation; legal to consult on regulatory and compliance aspects; and customer experience teams who will advocate for the voice of the customer and consider the impact on key metrics for all the changes you consider.

Organizational Design Models

Let's continue exploring the principles of organizational redesign by examining how traditional models can serve as frameworks for organizations embarking on a redesign with a focus on automation-first strategies.

The **McKinsey 7S model**,[4] encompassing strategy, structure, systems, shared values, skills, style, and staff, provides a universal approach to ensure internal alignment and effectiveness. This model is highly advantageous for organizations seeking to integrate new tech by promoting a cohesive, organization-wide assessment and plan (Figure 2.1).

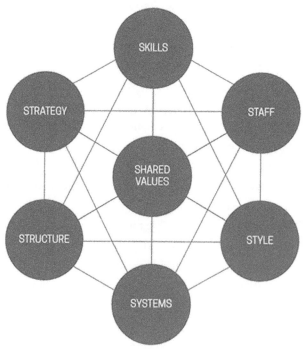

Figure 2.1 McKinsey 7S

Another influential model is the **SWOT analysis**, a tool assessing internal strengths and weaknesses alongside external opportunities and threats. It proves valuable for organizations aiming to gain a thorough understanding of both internal and external factors, facilitating the strategic integration of automation initiatives within these parameters (Figure 2.2).

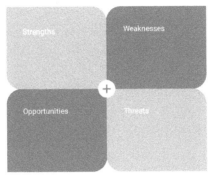

Figure 2.2 SWOT analysis

PESTLE analysis delves into macro-environmental factors—political, economic, social, technological, legal, and environmental. This model is particularly recommended for organizations who need to align their automation strategies with the broader environmental landscape (Figure 2.3).

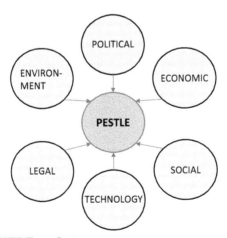

Figure 2.3 PESTLE analysis

The **Galbraith's star model** considers five key elements: strategy, structure, processes, rewards, and people. It ensures synergy among these components and is well-suited for organizations emphasizing the alignment of automation initiatives with the overall strategy and culture[5] (Figure 2.4).

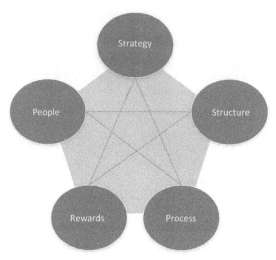

Figure 2.4 Galbraith's star model

The **Burke–Litwin model** offers a comprehensive framework exploring both external and internal factors, focusing on transformational elements like leadership, culture, and systems. It is particularly recommended for organizations that recognize the need for a radical redesign[6] (Figure 2.5).

Figure 2.5 Burke–Litwin model

McMillan's Fractal Web envisions organizations as interconnected webs connecting people, processes, systems, and entities and more, promoting flexibility, adaptability, and decentralized decision making. It is an ideal model for organizations who are splitting automation implementation between business functions rather than it being a centrally driven program, enabling multiple strategies and plans with an interconnected approach[7] (Figure 2.6).

Figure 2.6 McMillan Fractal Web

The **Weisbord six-box model** examines purpose, structure, relationships, rewards, leadership, and helpful mechanisms. Ensuring alignment with business goals, this model is recommended for organizations who want to combine the integration of technology with a people-focused approach to encourage a well-rounded and effective plan. In particular, rewards and incentives should not be overlooked when implementing any large change program affecting people[8] (Figure 2.7).

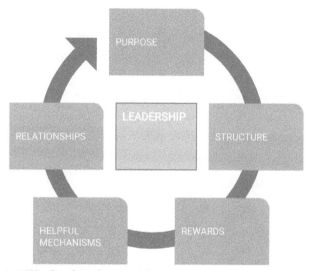

Figure 2.7 Weisbord six-box model

We'll discuss more recommendations on using these models in Chapter 6.

Potential Organizational Structures

In the realm of OD, selecting the right structure is paramount to embrace future of work trends and technology advances.

Traditional hierarchical structures, while offering clear lines of authority, might impede agility and responsiveness, which are crucial in the age of automation. A progressive organization should lean toward flatter structures, promoting a more agile and collaborative environment.

Traditional Hierarchical Structure

- **Definition:**
  - Classic setup with a clear chain of command from the top down. Each level of management oversees the one below.
- **Application:**
  - Provides stability and role clarity but might struggle in the fast-paced world of automation due to limited adaptability.

- **Recommendation:**
  - o If sticking with tradition, balance stability with the flexibility needed for automation. Key factors are clear communication, agile project methodologies, and adaptable leadership (Figure 2.8).

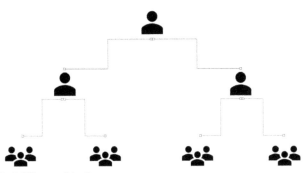

Figure 2.8 Hierarchical structure

Flat Organizational Structure

- **Definition:**
  - o Strips away layers of middle management promoting focused teams of experts, direct communication, quicker decision making, and increased agility.
- **Application:**
  - o Perfect for adapting swiftly to technological shifts, valuing collaboration, and innovation.
- **Recommendation:**
  - o Ideal for organizations seeking a responsive structure that drives innovation and cross-functional collaboration in automation initiatives (Figure 2.9).

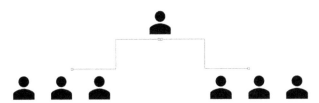

Figure 2.9 Flat structure

Specialist Networked Structure

- **Definition:**
  - o Envisions multiple business-led teams with a centralized hub of governance and standards. Combines autonomous central teams with teams of automation and AI specialists based in individual business functions dedicated to benefit realization.
- **Application:**
  - o Promotes a cohesive approach by harmonizing centralized governance with decentralized efforts. Ideal for scaling automation throughout the business.
- **Recommendation:**
  - • For organizations wanting both centralized guidance and distributed execution. Effective communication and alignment to agreed standards are crucial (Figure 2.10).

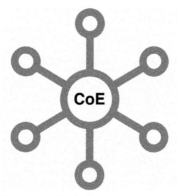

Figure 2.10 Specialist networked structure

Matrix Organizational Structure

- **Definition:**
  - o Combines functional and project-based structures, offering flexibility and specialization. Business functions align with specific automation or strategic projects.
- **Application:**

○ Accommodates diverse skill sets, enabling collaboration across functional silos and a focused approach to adopting the technology and use cases.

- **Recommendation:**
  - Recommended for balancing expertise with project-driven flexibility, enhancing efficiency in automation solutions (Figure 2.11).

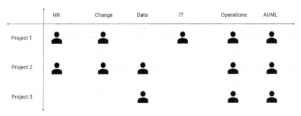

Figure 2.11 Matrix structure

Network-Based Organizational Structure

- **Definition:**
  - ○ Teams are grouped via a purpose, project, or initiative rather than traditional business function boundaries. This structure values collaboration and knowledge-sharing. Ideal for the interconnected nature of end-to-end automation solutions.
- **Application:**
  - ○ Encourages seamless collaboration essential for integrating diverse automation solutions, promoting adaptability and responsiveness.
- **Recommendation:**
  - ○ Suitable for organizations prioritizing cross-functional cooperation (Figure 2.12).

Figure 2.12 Network structure

Self-Managing Teams Structure

- **Definition:**
  - o Divides the organization into self-directed teams, each responsible for a specific task, region, or project, for example. Decision making is done within each team rather than directed by a single manager.
- **Application:**
  - o Encourages motivation, values expertise, and creates a sense of ownership among team members, aligning well with autonomy and creativity in AI and automation projects.
- **Recommendation:**
  - o Ideal for organizations with a skilled workforce and for empowering teams to experiment with the possibilities this technology can bring (Figure 2.13).

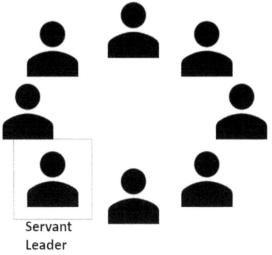

Servant
Leader

Figure 2.13 Self-managing teams structure

Co-Operative Ownership Structure

- **Definition:**
  - o Integrated model combining shared ownership, profit-sharing, financial transparency, and elected workers at the board level. This model also emphasizes self-managing teams but profit-sharing the benefits from automation makes this a more progressive structure.
- **Application:**
  - o Ideal for an automation-first redesign, aligning employees directly with financial and strategic goals and incentivizing success. Ensures workers have a say in both operational and strategic aspects as they collectively own the organization, actively contributing to strategic decision making.
- **Recommendation:**
  - o Requires a culture of shared responsibility, continuous learning, transparent communication, and robust collaboration channels between elected representatives and the leadership team (Figure 2.14).

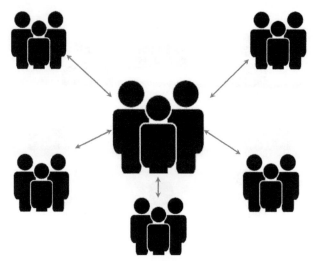

Figure 2.14 Co-operative owned structure

For an organization committed to radical redesign, a hybrid approach may be optimal. This involves combining elements of various structures, tailoring the design to the specific needs of the organization.

When you have a highly skilled workforce, self-managing teams are popular, they can work well when you have employees who are experts in their field and can set their own priorities and direction. But this may be something you transition to as we upskill our workforce. If you do decide to use self-managing teams make sure you "walk the walk" and don't deploy this with a traditional hierarchy of middle managers too; yes, I've seen this happen, as this will only engender cynicism and reduce autonomy and motivation. With self-managing teams, I would recommend inspirational leadership, performance coaches, and specialist leads, and then of course, trust in your people.

Self-managing teams can work in more sectors than technology and information workers, the book by Corporate Rebels *Make Work Fun* illustrates a powerful example of a care-at-home company Buurtzorg who dominate the care market in the Netherlands with thousands of self-managing teams of nurses. Decision making is done within each team, with coaches available, and policies that are made as simple as possible to focus on their core purpose. "True professionals know when and how to apply their competencies without the need for managers."[9]

The choice of structure should align with the organization's goals, culture, and the demands of an automation-first approach. It's about finding the right balance between clear leadership, efficient collaboration, and adaptability to thrive in an environment where technology plays a central role in shaping the future of work.

CHAPTER 3

Cognitive Computing as an Enabler for Change

When you're approaching organizational redesign, your transformation and journey will be unique. Transformation or redesign is not limited to large organizations that have the budgets to make huge investments in systems. It's possible to make a difference in the way any size organization works and redefine the workload, using cognitive computing as a transformative enabler.

So, whether you are new to artificial intelligence (AI) or an experienced and knowledgeable team bringing the benefits to your enterprise, it's always good to revisit and define what cognitive computing technology is and what it can do for you. After all, there's a lot of definitions floating around in the industry and it's good to start from a place of alignment.

What Is Cognitive Computing?

This technology is a game-changer for businesses. I think of it as an umbrella term for a group of advanced technologies that can mimic human brain power to boost efficiency, decision making, and overall flexibility.

This chapter breaks down the key ideas, parts, and uses of cognitive computing, giving you a thorough grasp of its importance in today's business world.

There's so much more to it and that really doesn't do it justice so let's take a deeper dive into the key components and their meanings.

Intelligent Automation (IA)

In simple terms, IA merges robotic process automation (RPA) with cognitive technologies such as machine learning (ML), and AI, among others, forming a smarter and more adaptable approach to automating in your business, giving you more advanced options to getting the work done.

Robotic Process Automation (RPA)

RPA acts like a digital assistant, handling the routine, electronic, rule-based tasks that can be repetitive and time-consuming. RPA is probably the most widely known and established component of IA.

Imagine it as a helpful virtual colleague that can be programmed to copy human actions on computers, reducing the need for manual efforts and improving overall accuracy. This technology allows employees to focus on more creative and complex aspects of their work, while RPA takes care of the routine and mundane tasks efficiently.

The robots, or digital co-workers, were built for this sole purpose, and unlike their human colleagues, they thrive on routine and manual tasks.

Artificial Intelligence (AI)

Imagine AI as the brains behind automation, incorporating ML, natural language processing (NLP), and computer vision. It's the brainpower that allows systems to not just follow instructions but to learn, understand language, and interpret visual information such as images and patterns.

Much like having a tech-savvy team member who can develop with experience, understand what you are communicating, and make thoughtful decisions based on the available data. It's hungry to learn from its mistakes and keen to put them right for the next interaction.

Imagine if automation had the power to not just complete routine tasks but to understand, learn, and tackle intricate challenges. That's what AI brings to the table—it transforms into a dynamic force, making systems adaptable and capable of handling tasks that require a level of understanding and complexity.

Generative AI

Generative AI is a type of AI that can generate new content, like text, images, or music, based on patterns and information they've learned from existing data. Imagine them as really smart robots that have read and analyzed tons of books, articles, and other information on the internet. Then, when you ask them to write a story or answer a question, they use what they've learned to generate a response that sounds like it could have come from a human. Remember how your phone does predictive text, or your Gmail suggests quick replies for you, this is done using ML that looks at how a human would typically respond and suggests the words for you.[1] But now it's been trained on much larger data sets, generative AI models can do this on a much larger scale.

However, it's important to understand that these models do not do research to provide accurate, factual information when generating responses. Instead, they rely on the vast amounts of data they were trained on, a large language model, to understand language patterns and predict and generate text that seems plausible. As a result, while these models can be incredibly helpful and produce high-quality text, they may not always provide accurate information, they are only predicting how a human might respond based on trends and patterns they've encountered. Factors such as errors or biases in the training data can lead to inaccuracies in the generated content. Therefore, it's essential for users to critically evaluate the information generated by these models and cross-reference it with reliable sources when accuracy is paramount.

IA can benefit by leveraging generative AI models to automate complex tasks that require humanlike reasoning and decision making. For instance, in financial services, combining generative AI with automation can enable systems to analyze unstructured data, such as customer feedback or market reports, and generate actionable insights, sentiment analysis, or recommendations for investment strategies.

It's also a perfect example of how IA is not just for big businesses; small businesses can thrive here too by incorporating generative AI into their work.

Machine Learning (ML)

Imagine ML algorithms as the tech version of learning to play chess from experience rather than starting with someone explicitly and laboriously teaching you every rule. It becomes a system that grows and becomes more proficient at tasks on its own. ML can get better at predictions or decisions by learning from experience, or from being given new data to learn from.

This adaptive way of learning is what makes IA solutions smart— they can navigate through elaborate situations and adapt to changing patterns, much like a team member who becomes more skilled with each task.

This capacity to learn and enhance on its own allows it to effectively manage tasks that demand adaptability and consistent enhancement over time.

ML acts like a sponge, soaking up information and knowledge, absorbing everything it can learn. ML algorithms can be trained using large data sets to make decisions autonomously, making them invaluable for various use cases such as predictive analytics, personalized recommendations, and anomaly detection.

Natural Language Processing and Generation

NLP is computers learning to understand and communicate using human language and speech patterns. It helps computers understand text, speech, and even emotions in language. For example, in IA, NLP can be used in chatbots to understand and respond to customer queries in natural language, making interactions more humanlike and efficient. Additionally, NLP can analyze large volumes of text data to extract valuable insights, such as customer feedback or market trends, helping organizations make informed decisions.

Process Mining

Process mining is software that allows us to see how processes actually work in an organization. It involves analyzing event logs and system data to understand how tasks are performed, identify inefficiencies, and optimize workflows. For instance, in IA, process mining can be used to visualize and analyze how tasks are executed in a business process, helping identify bottlenecks or deviations from the ideal process flow. This insight can then be used to identify use cases for automation that streamline the process and improve overall efficiency.

Intelligent Document Processing (IDP)

IA revolutionizes processing documentation by automating tasks such as data extraction, classification, and validation. This can significantly reduce manual effort and, crucially, minimize errors in workflows heavily reliant on documents.

By seamlessly handling document-related tasks, IDP takes the burden off human shoulders, making processes smoother and more error-free. This results in a work environment where employees can focus on more meaningful and impactful aspects.

Business Process Management (BPM)

BPM software can improve an organization's processes by optimizing and coordinating workflows. Unlike RPA, which automates specific tasks, BPM focuses on end-to-end process improvement by mapping, analyzing, and re-engineering how work flows across departments. BPM software uses tools like analytics and modeling to define current processes, identify inefficiencies, and implement more dynamic and effective workflows. By continuously refining these processes, we can improve operational efficiency, reduce costs, and quickly adapt to market changes and fluctuating demands.

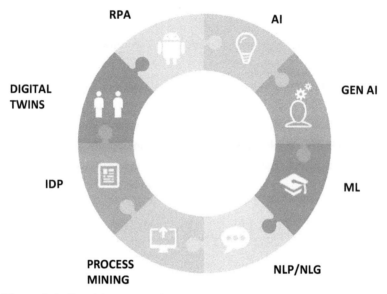

Figure 3.1 Cognitive computing

Digital Twin Technology

Digital twin technology is like creating a virtual clone of a physical object or system. It involves using real-time data and simulations to replicate the behavior and performance of a physical asset or process. For example, digital twin technology can be applied in manufacturing to create virtual replicas of production lines. These digital twins can simulate different operating conditions, predict equipment failures, and optimize production schedules, allowing organizations to minimize downtime and maximize efficiency. Another example is energy and utilities organizations, digital twins enable power plants and distribution networks to simulate various operating conditions, predict equipment failures, and optimize energy production and distribution. In smart cities, digital twins of urban infrastructure can monitor traffic flow, predict congestion, and optimize transportation systems to improve urban mobility and sustainability. Expanding the concept of digital twins to people, we can create virtual models that can predict human behavior and response, or in the health care world enable personalized diagnostics and treatment (Figure 3.1).

Harnessing Cognitive Technologies

Currently, IA brings us as close to mimicking the human brain as technology allows. As technology progresses, it will continue to get even closer to matching human intelligence. Gen AI is already bringing us along on that journey.

These uses bring the power of cognitive computing to life, utilizing the knowledge we have discussed such as AI, ML, and RPA. They are designed to address specific challenges, refine processes, and achieve business goals.

Visualize automating repetitive tasks, sharpening decision making through data insights, streamlining workflows, or introducing clever solutions in departments like customer service, finance, health care, and more.

When redesigning our organization, we are going to use cognitive computing to supercharge our operations—boosting efficiency, sparking innovation, and delivering positive outcomes.

Let's look at some uses for and the benefits in more detail.

Data Analysis and Insights

In practical terms, IA excels at managing extensive data. It efficiently processes large data sets, identifies crucial information, and detects patterns that may be challenging for humans to recognize. This capability plays a vital role in data-driven decision making, assisting organizations in confidently choosing the optimal path forward.

IA is your supersmart assistant, capable of handling vast amounts of information. Your high-tech sidekick if you will, sifting through data, pinpointing important patterns, and providing the best advice to simplify your work and enhance success.

Customer Service and Engagement

Using chatbots and virtual assistants, powered by IA and NLP, you can enhance customer interactions and employee experiences. They don't just offer swift responses; they customize recommendations specifically for you, ensuring a seamless and personalized user experience.

You gain immediate responses, personalized suggestions, and an experience that seems tailor-made for you. Like having a helpful assistant who understands your needs and responds instantly, taking on the heavy lifting and labor-intensive need to search for the response, giving you the chance to be more human with your customers and colleagues.

Process Optimization and Efficiency

Your business is now a well-oiled machine where IA is your skilled conductor, ensuring every step of your processes works together smoothly.

Implementing automation to optimize processes takes care of routine tasks, freeing up your human team to focus on the more interesting and impactful aspects of their work.

With the skilled training and knowledge you have provided to your digital co-workers, this ensures precision and consistency, reducing the chances of mistakes in critical processes. They will only work in the way you have trained them 100 percent of the time, there's no risk of human error, unless you train them to do so.

Predictive Analytics

If IA is your conductor then predictive analytics is your virtual strategic advisor who not only understands your business inside out but also has a crystal ball to foresee upcoming trends and challenges.

That's the power of leveraging ML within IA. You have a forward-thinking partner who sifts through vast data sets, identifies patterns, and predicts future market dynamics.

It's not just about steering clear of obstacles but seizing opportunities before they fully unfold. Visualize confidently navigating the business landscape with a foresight-driven decision-making compass.

This approach isn't just about making day-to-day operations smoother; it's about gaining a strategic edge in adapting to changes aptly. It's transforming challenges into actions for success, ensuring your organization stays one step ahead.

Enhanced Human Productivity

By automating mundane and repetitive tasks, IA empowers employees to focus on more meaningful and fulfilling aspects of their work. This enhances job satisfaction and taps into human creativity and problem-solving abilities. As a result, teams can contribute their unique talents to strategic initiatives, giving us a work environment that values individual contributions and promotes personal growth.

This means that employees get to do more of the work that excites and fulfills them, contributing their unique skills to exciting projects. Meanwhile, the organization benefits from a team that's not just productive, but also buzzing with creativity and innovation. It's a win-win that makes work more enjoyable and meaningful for everyone involved.

Cost Savings

By automating everyday tasks, we're not just making work easier; we're creating a smoother, more efficient operation. This not only saves time and effort but also ensures that things are done right the first time, preventing costly errors, and allowing resources to be directed toward more meaningful endeavors.

Strategic Decision Making

Our robot co-workers can go beyond just crunching numbers; they can empower organizations with meaningful insights drawn from data analysis.

The trustworthy guide that ensures decisions aren't just well-informed but also strategically in tune with the organization's larger goals, leading to meaningful success. This ensures that every strategic move is not only backed by data but also contributes significantly to the overall success and purpose of the organization.

Systems of Record, Collaboration, Engagement, and Productivity

As companies have progressed through their digital transformation journey, several different types of systems have emerged. Systems of record (SOR), systems of collaboration (SOC), systems of engagement (SOE), and systems of productivity and outcomes (SPO).[2] These systems collectively form the backbone of organizational operations, enabling seamless data management, real-time collaboration, personalized customer interactions, and performance optimization.

In this section, we will take a brief look at how cognitive computing can be used as an enabler in each.

Systems of Record (SOR)

SORs are databases or repositories where organizations store structured data related to their core business operations. They serve as the single source of truth for critical information and transactions, such as customer data, financial records, and inventory management. SORs are essential for maintaining data integrity and consistency.

Cognitive Computing Uses in Systems of Record

- Automate the process of capturing and entering data into the SOR from various sources to reduce manual errors and improve efficiency.
- Use intelligent algorithms to automatically validate and cleanse data stored in the SOR to ensure accuracy and reliability.
- Implement automated reporting and analytics tools to generate insights and drive data-driven decision making without manual intervention.
- Implement automated compliance checks and security measures to ensure data privacy and regulatory compliance within the SOR.

- Use BPM software to streamline processes and optimize workflows within the SOR, improving productivity and efficiency.
- Leverage predictive analytics to anticipate issues and optimize performance, enhancing operational efficiency and resource allocation.

Systems of Collaboration (SOC)

SOCs facilitate communication, information sharing, and collaboration among employees across different departments and locations. These systems enable real-time collaboration through features such as messaging, file sharing, video conferencing, and project management tools, enabling teamwork and innovation within organizations.

Cognitive Computing Uses in Systems of Collaboration

- Implement automation to send notifications and alerts to relevant team members based on predefined triggers or events, ensuring timely communication and task management.
- Implement intelligent assistants or chatbots to schedule and coordinate meetings, including finding suitable time slots and sending calendar invites, reducing administrative overhead.
- Use AI-powered systems to categorize and tag knowledge resources, such as documents and discussions, making it easier for employees to find relevant information and expertise.
- Integrate BPM with collaboration platforms to streamline approval processes, task assignments, and project workflows, increasing efficiency and accountability.
- Deploy AI assistants or chatbots within collaboration tools to provide instant support, answer queries, and facilitate interactions, enhancing productivity and user experience.
- Leverage process mining analytics to track collaboration patterns, identify bottlenecks, and measure team performance within

collaboration platforms, enabling continuous improvement and optimization.

Systems of Engagement (SOE)

SOEs focus on engaging customers, partners, and stakeholders through personalized interactions and experiences across various channels. These systems leverage customer data and insights to deliver tailored content, services, and support, driving customer satisfaction and loyalty.

Cognitive Computing Uses in Systems of Engagement

- Utilize ML algorithms to analyze customer preferences and behavior, delivering personalized content recommendations and product suggestions.
- Implement chatbots or virtual agents powered by NLP to provide automated customer support, such as answering queries, resolving issues, and handling routine tasks.
- Use predictive analytics to anticipate customer needs and behaviors, enabling proactive engagement and targeted marketing campaigns.
- Employ automation tools to schedule posts, monitor social media channels, and analyze engagement metrics, enhancing social media marketing and community management efforts.
- Integrate communication channels such as email, SMS, and chatbots to deliver consistent and seamless experiences across multiple touchpoints, improving customer engagement and satisfaction.
- Utilize NLP techniques to analyze customer feedback and sentiment across various channels, gaining actionable insights to enhance products and services.
- Automate the management of loyalty programs, including reward redemption, points tracking, and personalized offers.

Systems of Productivity and Outcomes (SPO)

SPOs aim to optimize core operations, drive performance, and achieve strategic business outcomes. Also known as enterprise resource planning systems, they integrate data, processes, and tools to get the work done and deliver measurable results across the organization.

Cognitive Computing Uses in Systems of Productivity and Outcomes

- Implement RPA to automate repetitive and manual tasks, such as data entry, report generation, and invoice processing, freeing up time for employees to focus on higher-value activities.
- Utilize analytics dashboards and performance metrics to monitor key performance indicators (KPIs), track progress toward goals, and identify areas for improvement in real time.
- Employ predictive maintenance algorithms to analyze equipment data and anticipate maintenance needs, minimizing downtime, and optimizing asset utilization.
- Use AI-powered algorithms to optimize supply chain operations, including inventory management, demand forecasting, and logistics planning, reducing costs, and improving delivery reliability.
- Develop decision support systems using digital twins, AI and ML to analyze data, simulate scenarios, and provide actionable insights to decision makers, enabling data-driven decision making.

Return on Investment (ROI)

Cognitive technology will be the dynamic force that reshapes organizations, it's more than just a tech tool—it's a guiding hand helping organizations create a new journey for how they're set up, how things work, and their big-picture plans. They inject innovation into how organizations see and shape their future. They help you go beyond just getting things done, they can redesign entire processes and improve the structure within which they operate.

I think it's important to address the elephant in the room, the usual argument that arises when we talk about using AI and automation: "Are the robots here to replace us?"

Let's not beat around the bush, there are some organizations that have utilized digital resources for this reason, to cut the bottom line. And yes, using IA for driving efficiency has traditionally been the main intention but as experience and knowledge have grown with the technology so has the creative way to use the tools. No longer just about efficiency, IA is a key player in the way you can redesign the way the organization works.

This utopia is all very exciting but requires investment, and of course, investment needs to come with the promise of return and in a time period that's going to be worthwhile for such a big shift in the way the organization is structured.

To achieve your ROI when implementing cognitive computing for organizational redesign, it's essential to maintain a watchful eye on the performance of your initiatives, ensuring they're delivering the goods. Regularly monitor a variety of KPIs to gauge their impact on your business outcomes. Dive into metrics such as how quickly processes are completed (process cycle time), the frequency of errors (error rates), the amount of money you're saving (cost savings), the increase in productivity across the board, how satisfied your customers and employees are, and whether your ROI is hitting the mark.

But don't stop there! Take all that important data you've collected and use it to fine-tune your strategies. Identify areas where things could be running smoother and faster, pinpoint bottlenecks that need clearing, and uncover opportunities for further optimization. This ongoing process of refinement is key to ensuring that your efforts are always aligned with your objectives and vision and are continuously evolving to meet the changing needs of your stakeholders.

And let's not forget about the importance of showcasing the added value you've generated. Use the insights gleaned from your performance monitoring to craft compelling communications that demonstrate the tangible benefits of AI and automation to your stakeholders. Whether it's showcasing significant cost savings, dramatic improvements in efficiency, or enhanced customer or employee satisfaction, painting a vivid picture of the positive impact will help garner support and buy-in from all parts of the business.

When it comes to IA programs, we're not just talking about a one-off project here. It's more like an ongoing journey where we're constantly tweaking and fine-tuning things to make practices better. You need to keep repeating and improving processes iteratively, incorporating technology as it advances along the way. That means paying attention to feedback from the team, analyzing any trends and insights that might pop up, and staying flexible to meet the ever-changing demands and needs of the business.

If we want to get the most out of cognitive computing while giving our organization a makeover, we must take a step back and look at the big picture. That's why it's important to follow the steps outlined in this book. That means we're not just diving in headfirst without a plan. We're taking a moment to sit down, map things out, and figure out the best way to make it work to ensure the right outcome is achieved. The big picture means we're not just focusing on one little piece of the puzzle—we're thinking about how all the different parts fit together.

And why are we doing all this? Well, because we want to maximize our ROI! We're not just taking an approach where we throw lots of money at the project and hope for the best; we need to be strategic about it. We're talking about real, tangible benefits here—things like improving speed to serve, being more flexible and adaptable, staying ahead of the competition, and just generally staying ahead of the game.

By embracing this tech we're not just making our organization better—we're enabling it to be the best it can be.

CHAPTER 4

What a Hyperautomation Organization Looks Like

We've established that robotic process automation is computers that look after the *doing* and intelligent automation combines that with artificial intelligence that can do the *thinking*.

But when I reference hyperautomation, I mean using a variety of cognitive computing capabilities to streamline as much of the business as possible, to run without human intervention.

Hyperautomation, that I might refer to interchangeably as *AI-first* or *automation-first*, allows for faster realization of our organization's objectives, vision, and enhanced productivity. It looks for ways to redesign the work being done with technology. You no longer take an existing process and automate tasks within it. Rather, you redesign the process completely, like you have a blank page, and fit your people around that process utilizing what your digital co-workers are good at, and what your people are good at.

This is a collaborative approach where you are utilizing humans and AI working together to meet the needs of your customers and employees, to keep your organization relevant in their field while ensuring it is running at optimum efficiency and cost (Figure 4.1).

So, what does this look like in action? Well, imagine you're dealing with a customer issue. Instead of having to jump through hoops and wait on hold forever, intelligent automation kicks in like an available worker to service your customer and satisfy their reason for contact using RPA and NLP, almost instantly. Should your customer need to talk to a person, there is no waiting on hold for hours as your call center team has been freed up from time-consuming administrative tasks so that they can provide a more personalized service when needed. Robots and humans are working together. And it's not just on the front lines

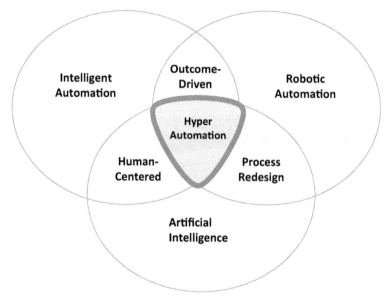

Figure 4.1 *Hyperautomation*

either—behind the scenes, automation is working hard to keep things running smoothly. Whether it's handling routine tasks, streamlining workflows, or crunching numbers and data, intelligent automation has got it covered picking up all rules-based processes.

And the best part ... because automation is woven into the fabric of the organization, you're not just efficient—you're optimum efficient! You can scale up at the drop of a hat, handling more customers, more transactions, more whatever-you-need, meaning you're able to flex to fluctuations in organization and industry demands.

It's a way of unifying your workforce by elevating humans and making the robots their digital co-workers who get the work done, interpret big data, provide strategic decision making and insights that will deliver maximum value realization. Employees are then freed and empowered to focus on high-value activities that require human creativity, problem-solving, relationship-building, and decision making, while routine tasks are automated to minimize manual effort and reduce errors. Collaboration between humans and machines is central to the organizational culture, with automation serving as a catalyst for innovation and continuous improvement. In this utopian vision of an automation-first organization, humans and AI work together harmoniously, leveraging each other's strengths to achieve common goals and drive sustainable growth and innovation.

Traditional automation often starts as a tactical, task-based model, where the focus is primarily on automating individual tasks or processes without considering the broader organizational objectives. This approach tends to address immediate pain points or inefficiencies without necessarily aligning with overarching business goals.

In contrast, hyperautomation emphasizes an outcome-based approach, where initiatives are strategically aligned with the end result in mind. Rather than just automating tasks in isolation, hyperautomation seeks to optimize entire workflows and end-to-end business processes spanning multiple business functions to achieve specific outcomes. By prioritizing the end goals and desired results, hyperautomation ensures that automation efforts drive measurable business value and contributes to long-term success. This shift from a task-based mindset to an outcome-based approach is essential for organizations looking for business transformation. It enables them to drive continuous improvement, innovation, and competitive advantage by focusing on delivering tangible business outcomes rather than simply automating isolated tasks.

The future of the workplace will involve a blurring of the lines between human and digital labor. This book should inspire you to work toward the day where the robots are an integral part of every team in your organization—a co-worker that can interact with your customers, accept work, move work between other robots, or to and from your people, completely autonomously and without human intervention into the platform. It will be able to learn from observing your activity, will give you access to (and insight from) data across new and legacy systems of record.

This is not a bleak, dystopian future where robots replace humans, quite the opposite—it is a future where your business can grow organically and efficiently by connecting the IT fabric of your entire organization and empower your workforce to trust and rely on their virtual colleagues, bringing to bear the skills required to augment and enhance their ability to deliver. This is a future that should be embraced, not feared.

This is why this book insists on placing humans at the center of the strategy. It emphasizes the importance of designing automation solutions that complement human capabilities, rather than replacing them. In a human-centric automation-first workplace, automation is not just about completing tasks faster; it's about empowering employees, utilizing human ingenuity, improving customer experiences, and driving business outcomes.

Adopting a human-centric hyperautomation approach brings a multitude of benefits, not only for the organization but also for its employees and society as a whole.

- **Employee happiness and well-being:** Embracing a human-centric hyperautomation strategy can significantly impact employee happiness and well-being. By automating mundane and repetitive tasks, employees can focus on more meaningful and fulfilling work that taps into their creativity, problem-solving skills, and emotional intelligence. This can lead to increased job satisfaction, reduced burnout, and higher morale among employees, contributing to a positive work environment.
- **Promoting lifelong learning:** Human-centric hyperautomation encourages a culture of continuous learning and development among employees. With automation handling repetitive tasks, employees have the opportunity to upskill and reskill, acquiring new and evolving knowledge and expertise to adapt to changing roles and technologies. This influences the educational agenda and curriculum for younger generations, preparing the workforce of the future for emerging job opportunities and ensuring a continued emphasis on lifelong learning.
- **Work–life balance:** By automating routine tasks, employees can reclaim valuable time that can be allocated to personal activities, family time, or pursuing hobbies and interests outside of work. This healthier work–life balance is essential for employee well-being, productivity, and overall satisfaction with their job and organization, which leads to talent retention.

- **Avoiding societal and economic disruptions**: A human-centric approach helps mitigate the potential negative impacts on society and the economy. By ensuring that automation solutions support rather than replace human labor, organizations can prevent mass job displacement and economic instability. Instead, we can create new opportunities for upskilling, reskilling, and job creation in emerging industries and sectors, fueling sustainable economic growth and prosperity.

- **Enhancing customer experiences:** Human-centric hyperautomation goes beyond efficiency gains and cost savings; it's also about delivering superior customer experiences. By leveraging automation to streamline processes and personalize interactions, organizations can enhance customer satisfaction, loyalty, and retention. Automation technologies like AI and ML enable organizations to anticipate customer needs, deliver proactive support, and tailor products and services to individual preferences, ultimately driving long-term value for both customers and the business.

- **Ethical considerations:** In the age of AI and automation, ethical considerations become increasingly important. Organizations need to prioritize ethical principles such as transparency, fairness, and accountability in the design and implementation. Organizations, and governments, must ensure that these technologies are used responsibly and ethically, with safeguards in place to prevent biases, discrimination, and unintended consequences. By embedding ethical considerations into the fabric of automation initiatives, organizations can build trust and uphold their reputation and integrity.

- **Driving innovation and creativity:** Contrary to the fear of automation stifling creativity and innovation, a human-centric approach can encourage a culture of innovation. By automating routine tasks, employees are freed up to explore new ideas, experiment with technologies and solutions, and collaborate across teams and departments. Technology becomes a catalyst for innovation, driving continuous improvement and disruptive thinking that fuels business growth and competitiveness.

Technology for Good

Look, I know I am a IT geek, I know I'm an optimist, and I do love the latest shiny gadget.

> But what have our gadgets actually accomplished? Over the last four decades, America saw an explosion of new technologies—from the internet to the iPhone, from Google to Facebook—but in that same period, the rate of poverty stagnated at a stubborn 13%, only to rise in the recent recession. So, a golden age of innovation in the world's most advanced country did nothing for our most prominent social ill.[1]

We know technology alone is not enough to save the world, or to drive success in your business, and that's why we're insisting on human-centric policies to utilize this tech.

Organizations that displace workers completely in favor of automation risk losing their greatest assets. Although there are good news stories out there in tech—the Ocean Cleanup project and solar glass to convert any window into a source of energy are two that come to mind—technology advances alone have not fixed the world's ills and inequalities. Therefore, a collective global intention to use AI and intelligent automation for good can uphold "Tech for Good" principles of empowering people, strengthening society, driving the economy, and protecting the planet.[2]

Technology can amplify human potential, but true progress is rooted in human wisdom, motivation, and creativity. By focusing on enhancing human potential rather than relying solely on technological solutions, human-centric hyperautomation advocates for a more balanced and effective approach to addressing organizational goals without causing further harm or disparities in the world.

Embracing this approach to hyperautomation is not just a strategic imperative for organizations; it's a moral and ethical responsibility. By prioritizing your people, mitigating societal and economic disruptions, upholding ethical principles, and driving innovation, organizations can unlock the full potential of automation while ensuring that humans remain at the heart of digital transformation.

Hyperautomation Use Cases

To understand the real-world applications of human-centric hyperautomation, let's explore some potential use cases from different industries:

Manufacturing

In the manufacturing industry, hyperautomation can revolutionize production processes. By automating tasks such as inventory management, quality control, and supply chain management, manufacturers can achieve higher operational efficiency, reduce costs, and ensure consistent product quality. RPA and AI-powered analytics can enable manufacturers to optimize their operations, enhance sustainability initiatives, and deliver products faster to meet customer demands. Human workers in this industry can then dedicate time to new products or techniques, research and development, and continuous improvement.

Health Care

In the health care sector, hyperautomation can have a profound impact on patient care and administrative processes. Automation technologies could improve the accuracy and speed of medical record management, appointment scheduling, and claims processing. This would allow health care employees to focus more on patient care, spend less time on administrative burdens, and enhance patient experiences. Machine learning and computer vision could be utilized to scan medical images such as X-rays, MRIs, and CT scans, to detect anomalies and assist in diagnosis. These advanced technologies can quickly analyze vast amounts of imaging data, identifying patterns and abnormalities that may be indicative of various medical conditions, improving the accuracy and speed of diagnosis, leading to earlier detection and more effective treatment strategies for patients.

Financial Services

In the financial services sector, adopting human-centric hyperautomation can transform operations while enhancing customer satisfaction. By leveraging RPA, AI, and ML technologies, institutions can automate tasks such as loan approvals, account reconciliation, and administration. They can use ML for fraud detection, risk analysis, automating compliance monitoring and reporting, facilitating adherence to regulations, and ensuring operational resilience. This frees up employees to focus on value-added activities like personalized customer interactions, strategic decision making and exploring how to utilize technology for further improvements.

Retail

In the retail sector, intelligent automation can transform both the customer shopping experience and backend operations. Retailers can use automation to personalize marketing campaigns, optimize inventory management, and streamline order fulfilment processes. For example, AI-powered engines analyze customer data to provide customized product recommendations, enhancing the shopping experience and driving sales. Additionally, robotic automation in warehouses automates tasks such as picking, packing, and sorting, enabling retailers to fulfill orders more efficiently and accurately. With automation handling routine tasks, retail staff can focus on delivering exceptional customer service, providing product expertise, and creating memorable in-store experiences that engineer customer loyalty.

Transportation and Logistics

In transportation and logistics, we can use hyperautomation for improving supply chain visibility, operational efficiency, and customer satisfaction. Automation can be used to optimize route planning, track shipments in real time, and automate freight forwarding processes and customs documentation. For instance, predictive analytics and sensors powered by internet of things enable logistics companies to anticipate demand, optimize delivery routes, reduce delays, and minimize transportation costs. With automation streamlining logistics operations, employees can dedicate their time to resolving complex logistical challenges, enhancing communication with clients, and developing innovative solutions even further to improve service quality and efficiency.

Hospitality and Tourism

In the hospitality and tourism industry, human-centric hyperautomation enables enhanced guest experiences by optimizing hotel operations and increasing revenue opportunities. Hotels and resorts can leverage automation to personalize guest services, automate check-in/out processes, and manage room inventory efficiently. Another example is AI-powered chatbots providing guests with instant assistance and recommendations, dinner reservations, room service or maintenance at the touch of a button, all automated as they're electronic tasks. This improves customer satisfaction and loyalty. Additionally, predictive analytics helps hoteliers forecast demand, adjust pricing strategies, and optimize room allocation to maximize revenue and occupancy rates. With automation handling administrative tasks, hospitality staff can focus on building genuine connections with guests, and delivering exceptional hospitality experiences that leave a lasting impression.

Public Sector and Government

Public sector and government agencies can use hyperautomation strategies to improve citizen services, enhance operational efficiency, and ensure regulatory compliance. For example, digital government platforms and chatbots provide residents with easy access to information and services, such as applying for permits, paying taxes, or accessing social benefits, all aimed at reducing administrative burdens and wait times. Employees in the public sector can utilize automation in regulatory compliance and auditing processes to help ensure transparency, accountability, and adherence to regulatory requirements, enhancing trust and confidence among citizens.

AI and ML enable predictive analytics and data-driven insights that allow policymakers to make informed decisions, allocate resources effectively, and address emerging challenges proactively, driving better outcomes for society as a whole. (Actually, could maybe someone remind politicians they should be trying to improve society, or shall we just go ahead and replace them first of all with democratic AI-driven bots, who won't take bribes, can take on vast amounts of factual data, can listen to constituent sentiments, and will never miss a vote?)

By automating repetitive administrative tasks and utilizing the resources saved, government employees can focus on providing responsive, citizen-centered services, invest in adult education upskilling programs, and deliver initiatives that provide positive social impact, equity, and social mobility.

The Future for Hyperautomation

As cognitive computing technologies continue to advance, the future of human-centric hyperautomation looks promising. Organizations that embrace a human-centric approach will be better positioned to navigate the evolving business landscape. Automation and AI will become more integrated into the fabric of organizations, with a focus on seamless collaboration between humans and machines. Benefits, such as increased efficiency, improved customer experiences, and empowered employees, will continue to drive its adoption across industries powering growth and prosperity. Increased profits will result in investments in innovation, and we'll continue to see more advances in organizations that adopt IA.

In the future, while technology will undoubtedly play a crucial role in streamlining processes and augmenting human capabilities, there are certain inherent qualities and skills that humans possess and will continue to be valued for. One of these is creativity—the ability to ideate, innovate, and think outside the box. Creativity is essential for problem-solving, design thinking, and envisioning novel solutions to complex challenges, areas where machines often struggle due to their reliance on predefined algorithms and existing, sometimes biased, data sets. Emotional intelligence and empathy are uniquely human traits that will always play a vital role in areas such as customer service, leadership, and teamwork. Humans possess the ability to understand and empathize with the emotions of others, leading to more meaningful connections and interactions. Additionally, critical thinking and judgment are indispensable skills for evaluating information, making ethical decisions, and navigating ambiguous situations, areas where human intuition and experience excel. Ultimately, the future of work will be characterized by a symbiotic relationship between humans and AI, where each leverages its unique strengths to achieve collective success.

As we look ahead, several trends and developments are likely to shape the future of human-centric hyperautomation. One significant trend is the increasing integration of automation technologies with fields such as augmented reality and virtual reality. Immersive technologies have the potential to transform how humans interact with systems, enabling more intuitive and natural user interfaces for controlling and monitoring automated processes. The rise of edge computing, quantum computing, and 5G networks is expected to accelerate the deployment of automation solutions enabling real-time data processing and decision making. Advances in AI and ethical AI frameworks will enhance transparency and accountability, addressing concerns around bias, privacy, and trust. Overall, the future of human-centric hyperautomation will be characterized by continuous innovation, collaboration, and a relentless focus on leveraging technology to enhance human capabilities and drive sustainable business outcomes.

The integration of advanced cognitive technologies will play a pivotal role in driving the success of hyperautomation initiatives. These technologies offer unprecedented capabilities to redesign complex processes, optimize workflows, and deliver superior business outcomes across various functions and departments. However, successful implementation requires more than just technology adoption; it necessitates a cultural shift, an aspirational strategy, cross-functional collaboration, and a commitment to continuous learning and improvement.

Organizations that want to remain resilient to these advances should already be considering how they can redesign their organization to adapt to this new world. Those that embrace cognitive technologies and value the potential of their people in the here and now, will be better positioned to thrive in the future of work.

CHAPTER 5

Strategic Aspirations for Intelligent Organizations

So, how do we make a case for using cognitive computing as the way to strategically transform and redesign the organization?

You need to define your aspirations, goals, plans, and desires to keep yourself ahead of all your competitors and give you that special edge. After all, who doesn't want to be the first to make waves in their industry?

This starts with your overall vision. You need a vision to be able to move forward. The vision statement's intention is to set out the aspirations of the organization that will enable them to deliver their goals and ambitions. It's a powerful statement that inspires everyone involved by expressing what the organization hopes to achieve in the long run. It's about painting a vivid picture of where the organization wants to go and what it wants to accomplish, uniting everyone around a common goal.

This is why your vision is your guiding star for what you want to achieve as an organization in a defined timeline.

Previously, a management consultant might have told you that visions are delivered over a three- to five-year period, but when it comes to something like a full organizational redesign using cognitive computing, this will need to either be a shorter time period or reviewed annually to ensure that you're not outdating your plans due to the ever-changing nature of this technology.

The vision articulates the value in embarking on organizational redesign. The vision should embrace an automation-first mindset, aiming to empower the human workforce for more value-driven business initiatives, leveraging human strengths like relationship building and empathetic decision making.

Be specific about what the technology will bring to the table in terms of transformation. Ensure that your vision contains things only you can deliver.Make it realistic so that it can be achieved, but also so that the organization fully buys into this. And be sure you are transparent on what you want to achieve and how you plan to deliver this. Lastly set milestones to review and adapt the vision if needed or the relevance changes.

Let's take a look at what an example vision for organizational redesign could look like....

We want to achieve the following by

1. We will redesign the way the organization is servicing our customers to ensure we are increasing our speed of delivering customer service by x percent.
2. We will utilize an automation-first mindset to redesign our working practices to fully move toward a collaborative workforce of intelligent automation working with our employees.
3. We will increase our cognitive computing tool kit and our knowledge on how these tools can make a difference in the way our organization operates, so we can grow our competitive edge and impact the bottom line with improvements of x percent.
4. We will create a no fear, automation-first approach to change within the organization. Giving our employees the creative space to be innovative in their approach to how to redesign their ways of working. Nothing is off the table when considering how to improve customer service.
5. We will introduce an approach to ongoing continuous improvement in the new redesigned world. Making sure we are committed to continue to drive the right practices, regularly review the ways of working, and implement changes to keep the organization at its best.

While determining what your vision should and could be, you'll need to understand your scope and remit. It's easy to get ahead of yourself and set a challenge to hugely redefine the whole organization, but this can leave you overwhelmed, create a lengthy change cycle, and, culturally, this might not be right to use a "big bang" approach.

This is why it's an important part of your journey to set your short-term goals along with your overall longer term strategic vision. A short-term goal is a target you aim to accomplish soon, typically within a shorter but realistic timeframe. These goals often serve as building blocks toward the larger vision.

They're also useful for tackling smaller projects or ideas. Consequently, short-term goals are usually more attainable and can spur momentum toward bigger accomplishments.

So, what should your short-term goals look like to ensure they are supporting your transformational growth journey and helping you redesign your ways of working? Let's walk through some steps to consider when setting your short-term goals and how these will impact your plans to transform your organization.

- **Have your long-term plan in mind:** This is why you should set your vision first! This sets your stake in the ground and then you can break down the vision into your short-term goals to enable you to achieve what you need to deliver and really transform the way things are done.
- **Now work backwards:** Now you know what you want to achieve, the how to achieve it needs to be defined. Work back from the long-term plan and detail the steps that are needed to get there. These steps are the foundations of your short-term goals or objectives.
- **Know the difference between process and outcome goals:** Knowing the difference between process and outcome goals is key when setting targets. Process goals are all about the steps you take to get where you want to be, while outcome goals are the specific results you're aiming for. So, think of process goals as your roadmap, showing you the way, and outcome goals as your final destination.
- **Don't try to bite off more than you can chew:** Trying to do too much at once can hinder progress and buy-in. When it comes to setting short-term goals, it's essential to break down the big tasks into smaller, manageable chunks. These bite-sized objectives allow for a more focused and achievable approach, making progress feel more tangible and motivating. By tackling

one step at a time, you'll build momentum and stay on track toward reaching your longer-term goals and overall vision.

- **Track, track, track:** Tracking the progress and outcomes of your short-term goals is essential for several reasons. First, it provides clarity and direction, helping you stay focused on what needs to be done. Secondly, it allows you to identify any obstacles or challenges that may arise along the way, enabling you to address them promptly. Additionally, tracking your goals allows you to celebrate your achievements and milestones, which can boost morale and motivation. Tracking will provide valuable feedback on the effectiveness of your strategies, allowing you to make necessary adjustments for better results in the future.

- **Share away:** Don't be shy! Share what it is you're looking to do and what needs to happen in order to achieve it. Your organization will have a wealth of resources, knowledge, and experience that may aid you to achieve your short-term goals and eventually your long-term vision. Also, by sharing what you are doing you might be highlighting if someone else has similar plans and therefore reducing duplication of effort.

- **Consider those blockers:** When setting short-term goals, it's crucial to consider potential blockers that could hinder your progress. These blockers can include anything from lack of resources to unforeseen circumstances. By anticipating these obstacles upfront, you can develop approaches to overcome them more effectively. Whether it's allocating additional resources, seeking assistance, or adjusting your approach, acknowledging, and addressing potential blockers in your goal-setting process can help ensure smoother progress and increase your chances of success.

Let's have a look at some examples of short-term goals in organizational redesign.

- Implementing a new process to enhance efficiency or productivity, resulting in noticeable time or cost savings.

- Conducting a trial or test phase for a new technology or system, demonstrating its effectiveness and potential value to the organization.
- Analyze customer data to understand the common themes that are causing customer complaints and align these to processes that need to be redesigned to improve customer sentiment.
- Garnering support for change initiatives by identifying and engaging early adopters and champions within the organization.

Now we have the long- and short-term goals, let's dive into our redesign strategy.

Design Thinking

How can you think about the bigger picture and use a design thinking approach to your organizational redesign?

Design thinking refers to using the principles and methodologies of design thinking with the process of reshaping and improving the structure, processes, and culture of the organization.

Let's approach this like you are ripping up the rule book, nothing is off the table to consider when redesigning. If you had a blank sheet of paper to design what your organization looks like, design thinking is the approach to use.

Design thinking is a problem-solving method but with a twist—it's all about putting your people first. When you use it for organizational redesign, you're conducting a deep dive into what makes your team, your customers, and everyone else tick.

Armed with this deep understanding, you're ready to get creative. You brainstorm ideas, bounce them around with your team, and explore all sorts of possibilities. In a workshop environment where every idea is welcome, no matter how "out there" it may seem. This free-flowing creativity is where you can be truly innovative and think outside the box for transformation.

But it's not just about producing creative new ideas just for the sake of it. Each idea is formed with the intention to solve real problems and make meaningful improvements. You're looking for opportunities to streamline processes, enhance customer experiences, and make life easier for everyone involved.

The best part about this approach is it's all about collaboration. You're not doing this alone—you're working together with your team, your customers, and your stakeholders every step of the way. It's a big brainstorming session where everyone's input is valued, and together, you're shaping the future of your organization. Remember the *day in the office* example in Chapter 1; they were taking a design thinking approach.

So, whether you're redesigning your workflows, rethinking your products, or overhauling your customer service, design thinking is there to guide you in a new direction; a roadmap that helps you navigate the twists and turns of organizational redesign, ensuring that every decision you make is rooted in empathy, creativity, and collaboration.

Design thinking for organizational redesign typically involves several key stages:

1. **Understand:** To kick off your organizational redesign journey, dive deep into the day-to-day experiences and perspectives of everyone involved—your team members to your customer base and influential stakeholders. This goes beyond just surface-level chats; it's about immersing yourself fully in their world. Spend time observing their workflows, engage in meaningful conversations to uncover pain points, and actively seek out their ideas for improvement, this is what really matters to them. What specific tasks do they find laborious and time-consuming? Where do they see room for growth and improvement? By truly understanding their daily realities and gaining insights into their challenges and aspirations, you'll gain invaluable knowledge that will lay the groundwork for your redesign plans.

2. **Define:** Now that you've taken a good look at what's bugging people and where there's room to improve, it's time to map out your goals. What's the ultimate aim of this redesign? Maybe you're looking to reduce those time-wasting processes that have everyone pulling their hair out, tighten up quality control to slash unnecessary errors that keep cropping up, or drive better

customer experience to ensure they keep coming back to you. Whatever your goals, make sure it's crystal clear, something you can measure with real numbers, and totally in sync with the organization's long-term goals and strategy.

3. **Brainstorm:** Now's the perfect time to ignite those sparks of creativity! Gather a diverse group of individuals from various departments within the organization, or even a focus group involving your customers or users. Together you can explore what are your most important problems to solve. This presents an opportunity to go beyond conventional restrictions and open up a whole new set of prospects to you. Consider the potential applications: AI-powered chatbots adept at anticipating customer needs, robotic processes executing tasks with remarkable efficiency, or warehouse sensors optimizing operations seamlessly. Embrace the freedom to creatively discover innovative solutions, regardless of their initial complexity.

4. **Prototype:** Time to roll up your sleeves and put your ideas to the test. Build prototypes or mock-ups of your solutions and see how they fare in the real world. This might involve setting up pilot projects, running simulations, or even just sketching out rough designs on paper. The goal here is to quickly iterate and refine your ideas based on feedback from users.

5. **Test:** Once you've got some prototypes ready to go, it's time to see how they hold up in reality. Put them in front of real users and gather feedback on what works and what doesn't. Are the solutions intuitive to use? Do they solve the problems they were designed for? Use this feedback to fine-tune your designs and make them even better.

6. **Implement:** With your designs refined and validated, it's time to put them into action. Roll out your AI or automation solutions across the organization, making sure to provide plenty of support and training to help everyone get up to speed. And don't forget to celebrate your successes along the way!

7. **Iterate:** The work doesn't stop once your solutions are live. Keep a close eye on how they're performing and be ready to adjust

UNDERSTAND   DEFINE   BRAINSTORM   PROTOTYPE   TEST   IMPLEMENT   ITERATE

Figure 5.1 Design thinking

as needed. Maybe there are new opportunities for automation that you hadn't thought of before, or perhaps some tweaks are needed to make existing solutions even more effective, trend analysis is your biggest ally here. By staying flexible and open to change, you'll ensure that your organization continues to evolve and thrive in the automation-first world (Figure 5.1).

CHAPTER 6

Assessing the Organization for Redesign

Successful implementation of cognitive computing requires a comprehensive understanding of the organization's current state before we can build a strategic plan for future transformation. This chapter will provide you with a variety of ways to do that.

Internal Assessment

An internal assessment focuses on evaluating various aspects of the organization, including systems, infrastructure, people, processes, data, culture, and skills. It aims to answer key questions such as:

- How well do the existing systems and infrastructure support the organization's vision and strategy?
- Are there any legacy systems that need replacement or infrastructure changes required to enable your new initiatives?
- What are the current skill sets within the organization, and what additional training or hiring may be necessary?
- How do the existing processes align with the desired future state of automation?
- Is the organizational culture conducive to embracing the technology and driving change?
- What is the current state of the organization's data architecture and governance?
- How accessible and reliable is the organization's data for decision-making and assessing automation feasibility?
- Are there any bottlenecks or inefficiencies in our current ways of working?

- What mechanisms and channels are in place for feedback and communication?
- How scalable are the organization's current processes and systems to accommodate future growth?
- What resources and budget allocations are available for investing in cognitive technologies and training programs?
- How well-integrated are different departments and teams within the organization?
- What metrics or key performance indicators are currently being used to measure the effectiveness of operations?

External Assessment

Organizations should also evaluate the external factors that could impact their automation initiatives, to ensure that their strategies are aligned with the broader industry landscape, as well as foresee any challenges that we may need to consider or address.

Market and Competition Analysis

- Assess competitors' strategies, strengths, weaknesses, and capabilities to identify market gaps, potential threats, or opportunities for differentiation.
- Assess market trends, emerging technologies, and industry practices to understand any evolving market demands.
- Research how competitors have implemented artificial intelligence (AI) or automation and the results they have achieved.

Reputation and Customer Alignment

- Utilize external reviews and customer feedback to assess perceptions of the current reputation, trustworthiness, and credibility of your organization.
- Conduct customer research and leverage data analytics to gain insights into customer preferences and current pain points.

- Analyze customer segments and their unique needs to determine the factors most important to them about your service or products.
- Consider how societal and public perception of automation technologies may influence customer behavior, market preferences, and whether this may vary across different regions or demographics.

Technology Assessment

- Research emerging technologies relevant to your organization's industry.
- Assess the suitability of partnerships, or outsourcing options compared to in-house development.
- Research what data protection regulations and industry standards are in place to safeguard sensitive information used in automation processes.
- Research the current threat and breaches in other similar organizations relating to cybersecurity measures and data privacy protocols to assess the organization's resilience.
- Assess suitable intelligent automation vendors to ascertain suitability for your requirements, infrastructure, and other key aspects such as support offered.

Political, Legal, and Regulatory

- Assess the political landscape to understand how government policies and regulations may affect the organization's operations and ways of working.
- Consider factors such as trade agreements, taxation policies, and political stability.
- Conduct a thorough review of industry-specific regulations, compliance standards, and legal requirements.

Talent and Skills Availability

- Evaluate the availability of skilled talent and expertise in the labor market, locally and globally, relevant to your chosen technology.
- Gain a thorough understanding of benchmarked salaries and benefits to determine if your organization is competitive enough to attract and retain top talent.

Economic Landscape

- Analyze economic trends, such as market fluctuations, inflation rates, and economic growth forecasts, to anticipate how changes in the economy may impact the organization's financial resources and investment decisions related to automation.
- Evaluate the organization's financial stability and liquidity to determine its capacity for investing in automation technologies and initiatives.

Conducting a Gap Analysis

Once the internal and external assessments are complete, you can conduct a gap analysis to identify the disparity between the current state and the desired future state. We need to understand what factors from our current state support our automation-first vision and what does not.

Compile the findings of the assessment into a comprehensive report providing a clear overview of the current state to set the stage for identifying areas for improvement. Comparing the organization's current capabilities, processes, and systems with the envisioned future state should highlight the gaps between where the organization stands today and where it aims to be in terms of readiness, operational efficiency, and strategic alignment. This comparison will help prioritize areas for intervention and investment.

Distinguish between the base level requirements necessary to meet minimum standards for implementation and the aspirational level representing the organization's ideal state—closing the gap might need to be a staged approach. Define clear objectives and metrics for both levels, ensuring alignment with strategic goals and priorities. This differentiation allows you to prioritize initiatives based on their potential impact and feasibility.

Once the gaps are apparent, evaluate the potential benefits of closing each gap, any associated risks, and the level of effort required. This needs to be communicated and agreed upon with key stakeholders before we move on to our action plan that will seek to close these gaps.

Creating an Action Plan

We can now assimilate insights from the various assessments and activities we've done so far, including the comprehensive gap analysis, any risk analysis, and any actions identified for a project plan. We'll also include actions from our change management plan, skill gaps analysis, and role mapping exercise that we'll explore in more detail in subsequent chapters. Our action plan will guide us toward our desired future state.

With such a lot of data in this action plan, we should agree on how we will prioritize. We scrutinize each potential action, weighing its potential impact against the organization's strategic objectives. Each initiative must have a clearly defined objective and a realistic timeline. Prioritize any quick wins with a short deadline.

Actions need an owner, with leadership, change agents, project managers, automation Centre of Excellence (CoE) team members, and business function leaders ready to pick up relevant actions. We also need to consult on what tools and resources they need to succeed.

We should then establish a robust monitoring mechanism with regular reviews and checkpoints allowing us to review feedback, track actions, optimize, and refine. We remain agile, ready to adapt, and renew our collective ambition to achieve our vision.

Assessing and Anticipating Pitfalls and Challenges

While the benefits of human-centric automation are compelling, in our planning phase, we must be prepared to address several challenges and pitfalls that are often seen, to help ensure a successful implementation.

1. AI algorithms used in human-centric automation rely on data to make decisions. However, these algorithms can be biased if the training data are not diverse or representative of real-world scenarios. Regular audits need to be planned to be vigilant in monitoring AI models to identify and address any biases that may arise.

2. If you are planning on using large language models (LLM) and generative AI in your automation solutions, you need to consider and weigh up whether you need to purchase licenses for your own private LLM, or build your own, to ensure that any information entered into them remains under your control and ownership.

3. Factor in the time it will take to establish a center of excellence and how long it will be before they are skilled enough to start showing impact.

4. Automation has the potential to displace certain job roles, raising concerns about job security and diminishing the desire to execute the changes required. Organizations must proactively address these concerns by implementing strategies for retraining and redeploying employees whose roles may be impacted as well as relying heavily on change management and incentives to facilitate this.

When assessing the challenges you are likely to face, it is good practice to anticipate your response and mitigation methods. Viewing these through the lens of the **CHIN model** can help you prepare and handle any obstacles along the way.

1. **Control**: assess the ability to control internal and external factors for the issue at hand. For this issue, are you able to control the impact on the strategy or performance?

2. **Help**: identify areas where external expertise or support may be required. For this issue, are there known parties who can help you overcome the challenge?

3. **Influence**: evaluate the team or organization's ability to influence stakeholders and key decision makers. For this issue, are there known parties who will advocate, support, and endorse proposed changes to influence a successful outcome?

4. **Noise**: anything we can't control, help, or influence is just noise to be ignored or to be quietened. For this issue, are there sources of distraction that can be ignored, mitigated, or communicated in order to quieten the impact?

Using Established Organizational Design Techniques

In Chapter 2, we discussed the different organizational models that can help you with assessments for organizational design. Please revisit that section for an explanation of each, but let's explore further which, in my opinion, fits best with an organizational redesign to become automation-first.

McKinsey 7S Model (see Figure 2.1)

- **Advantages:** provides a complete view of the organization, ensuring alignment between strategy, structure, systems, and culture. Simple for organization-wide assessment and planning. Helps identify potential areas of misalignment that could hinder automation implementation.
- **Disadvantages:** focuses primarily on internal factors and may not adequately consider external aspects or technological advancements.
- **Recommended steps to execute:**
  - Start by convening a cross-functional team representing various departments within the organization.
  - Identify and assess each of the seven elements (strategy, structure, systems, shared values, skills, style, and staff) using surveys, data, expert interviews, and observations.
  - Develop an action plan to address any gaps or inconsistencies identified, ensuring that automation initiatives are integrated seamlessly with the overall organizational strategy.

SWOT Analysis (see Figure 2.2)

- **Advantages:** offers a comprehensive view of internal strengths and weaknesses, as well as external opportunities and threats. Provides a structured framework for strategic decision making and prioritization.
- **Disadvantages:**
  o Relies heavily on subjective assessments and may be influenced by biases.
  o Does not provide specific guidance on how to address identified weaknesses or threats.
- **Recommended steps to execute:**
  o Gather key stakeholders from different departments to conduct a thorough analysis of each category, using data-driven insights and research to validate findings.
  o Prioritize the most significant factors identified in each category, considering their potential impact on automation initiatives.
  o Develop strategies to leverage strengths and opportunities while mitigating weaknesses and threats, aligning them with the program vision.

PESTLE Analysis (see Figure 2.3)

- **Advantages:** explores macro-environmental factors that may impact automation initiatives, offering insights into broader societal, technological, and regulatory trends. Helps organizations anticipate and adapt to external changes.
- **Disadvantages:**
  o May overlook internal dynamics and focus too heavily on external factors.
  o Requires significant effort and resources to gather and analyze data on political, economic, social, technological, legal, and environmental factors.
- **Recommended steps to execute:**

- o Research and gather information on all these factors relevant to your AI and automation initiatives, avoiding opinion and conjecture.
- o Analyze each factor individually, assessing its potential impact on your strategy and identifying potential risks and opportunities.
- o Develop contingency plans and adaptation strategies to address potential challenges and capitalize on emerging opportunities.

Galbraith Star Model (see Figure 2.4)

- **Advantages:** emphasizes the alignment of technology projects with strategy, structure, and culture. Helps identify and address gaps in key areas such as processes, rewards, and people. Provides a clear framework for designing and implementing an automation program that supports human-centric objectives.
- **Disadvantages:** overlooks the importance of assessing systems, an aspect crucial to tech projects. May not fully capture the complexity of large or decentralized organizations.
- **Recommended steps to execute:**
  - o Evaluate the current organizational structure, processes, and reward systems to identify areas that support or hinder automation objectives.
  - o Develop and implement changes to align these factors with automation strategy, promoting synergy and coherence.
  - o Monitor and adjust the implementation of automation initiatives as needed to reach the desired state.

Burke Litwin Model (see Figure 2.5)

- **Advantages:** offers a framework for assessing transformational change and helps understand the drivers of change to develop targeted strategies.
- **Disadvantages:** can be complex and difficult to implement without proper expertise or resources.

- **Recommended steps to execute:**
    o Conduct a comprehensive assessment of all factors using a combination of quantitative and qualitative data.
    o Identify key transformational factors such as leadership, culture, and systems that are critical to the success of automation initiatives.
    o Develop a detailed action plan to address any barriers or obstacles identified, focusing on creating a supportive environment for adoption.
    o Monitor the implementation of automation initiatives closely, measuring their impact on organizational performance and adjusting strategies as needed to ensure continued progress.

McMillan's Fractal Web (see Figure 2.6)

- **Advantages:**
    o Envisions organizations as interconnected webs, promoting flexibility and adaptability.
    o Supports decentralized decision making and distributed leadership. Allows for multiple strategies and plans with an interconnected approach, accommodating organization-wide automation initiatives.
- **Disadvantages:** may lead to ambiguity or confusion in roles and responsibilities, particularly in large or complex organizations. Requires robust communication and coordination mechanisms to ensure coherence and alignment across the organization.
- **Recommended steps to execute:**
    o Visually map the organization as an interconnected web of relationships and interactions, identifying key nodes and connections that influence automation initiatives.
    o Encourage decentralization and distributed decision making to support agility and adaptability.
    o Develop clear communication channels and collaboration platforms to facilitate information sharing and coordination across different business functions and teams.

- o Monitor the interconnectedness of different nodes and relationships within the organization, identifying areas for improvement and optimization.

Weisbord 6 Box Model (see Figure 2.7)

- **Advantages:**
  - o Examines key elements such as purpose, structure, relationships, and leadership, providing a comprehensive view of organizational effectiveness. Emphasizes the integration of rewards and incentives with automation initiatives, encouraging alignment with strategic objectives.
  - o Helps organizations identify areas for improvement and develop targeted interventions to support automation transformation.
- **Disadvantages:** heavily focuses on values and people which makes it good for cultural change, it can ignore more technical elements such as systems and processes that are required for digital change projects.
- **Recommended steps to execute:**
  - o Assess each of the six key elements in relation to your goals and objectives.
  - o Identify areas of alignment and misalignment between these elements and automation initiatives, focusing on areas that require attention or improvement.
  - o Develop targeted interventions to address any gaps or inconsistencies identified, such as updating reward systems or improving communication channels.
  - o Monitor the impact of these interventions on automation adoption and effectiveness, adjusting strategies as needed.

You can see that, yet again, there would be no *one size fits all* approach and a combination of techniques to assess your organizational landscape could be needed.

Let's have a look at some fictional case studies to see different techniques in action to highlight how a thorough organizational assessment can illuminate a clear the path to realization of AI and automation benefits.

Case Study: Transformation of Retail Chain XYZ Into an Automation-First Business

Introduction: Retail Chain XYZ is a prominent player in the luxury consumer goods industry with over a century of trading history, operating with multiple retail stores and a central head office. They are embarking on a radical organizational redesign to become an automation-first business, integrating AI, machine learning, and automation into every process. Despite having some basic automation processes in place, such as emailing invoices and purchase orders, they are relatively new to the concept and seek to overhaul and modernize their entire business model.

The following are the results of their organizational assessments utilizing the Galbraith Star Model, SWOT analysis, action planning, process analysis, and risk analysis.

Galbraith Star Model

Strategy: XYZ's current strategy focuses on traditional retail operations and growth. While there is a clear direction for expanding market presence and improving customer experience, the existing strategy does not adequately prioritize or invest in key areas for automation such as inventory management and targeted marketing. However, the emphasis on growth and operational efficiency aligns well with the goals of transitioning to an automation-first business model.

Structure: the organizational structure of XYZ is hierarchical, with clear reporting lines and departmental silos. While this structure may have served the company well in the past, it may not be conducive to agile decision making and cross-functional collaboration required for successful end-to-end automation. However, the presence of established departments and roles provides a foundation that can be leveraged to support automation initiatives with some restructuring and realignment.

Processes: XYZ's current processes are predominantly manual, with limited automation in place for routine tasks such as invoicing. While this currently results in inefficiencies, it also presents an opportunity for significant improvement through automation, especially for inventory management and reporting. Upgrading existing systems is critical to optimize these processes. This will likely entail adopting a cloud-based automation platform capable of integrating with the organization's existing enterprise resource planning and customer relationship management systems. Additionally, deploying AI and machine learning algorithms into processes could optimize inventory management, pricing strategies, and personalized marketing efforts.

Rewards and incentives: the existing rewards and incentives at XYZ are primarily based on sales performance and customer satisfaction metrics. While these metrics are important for business success, there will need to be recognition and incentives specifically tied to automation-related achievements. However, the culture of performance-based rewards aligns well with the goal of powering innovation and driving automation adoption.

People: employee training and development efforts focus on enhancing product knowledge, sales skills, and customer service. While there may not yet be training programs specifically tailored to digital skills, the company demonstrates a commitment to investing in employee growth and development. This foundation can be leveraged to provide targeted training and upskilling opportunities for employees to support automation initiatives effectively.

Leadership: leadership at XYZ exhibits a strong focus on driving business growth and maintaining operational excellence. There is a tendency for the majority of decision making and approvals to escalate to leadership, which employees perceive as a bottleneck. This approach will likely need rethinking to enable a culture of autonomy and empowerment. The leadership's vision and commitment to organizational success, coupled with the high regard in which they are largely held, does provide a solid foundation for transitioning to an automation-first business model.

SWOT Analysis

Strengths

- Established brand presence and customer loyalty.
- Access to extensive customer data that could be used for personalization and targeted marketing.
- Willingness to embrace change and invest in technology.
- Low turnover and high employee satisfaction.

Weaknesses

- Limited experience and expertise in automation technologies.
- Resistance to change among some employees.
- Lack of comprehensive data infrastructure for AI and machine learning applications.
- Potential disruptions to existing workflows during the transition phase.

Opportunities

- Enhanced operational efficiency and cost savings through automation.
- Improved customer experience through personalized recommendations and streamlined processes.
- Expansion of online and omnichannel retail capabilities.
- Potential for new revenue streams through data monetization and predictive analytics.

Threats

- Competition from tech-savvy rivals and disruptors in the retail industry.
- Data privacy and security concerns associated with AI and machine learning applications.
- Regulatory challenges related to data governance and compliance.
- Dependence on external vendors and technology partners for automation solutions.

Short-Term Action Plan

- Conduct a comprehensive assessment of current processes and identify areas with the most impact.
- Develop a roadmap for implementing intelligent automation, prioritizing the quick wins.
- Invest in employee training programs to build skills in AI, machine learning, and automation technologies.
- Pilot test solutions to evaluate their effectiveness and gather feedback.

Long-Term Action Plan

- Scale up successful automation initiatives across all retail stores and business functions.
- Forge strategic partnerships with technology vendors specializing in automation solutions.
- Build a robust data infrastructure to support advanced analytics and machine learning algorithms.
- Drive a culture of continuous innovation and experimentation, encouraging employees to explore new automation opportunities.
- Monitor industry trends and emerging technologies to stay ahead of the curve and maintain a competitive edge in the market.

XYZ Process Heatmap

Processes have been assessed for their feasibility to be redesigned using cognitive technology. (See Table 6.1)

Prioritization

For the processes that have been identified as high feasibility, the key stakeholders have discussed and made a judgment on the simplicity of the process and its potential business impact. This assessment will result in the prioritization of the automations that land in the golden circle (Figure 6.1).

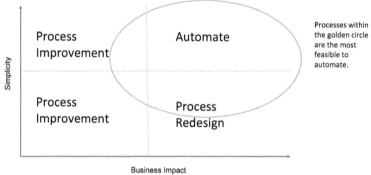

Figure 6.1. Automation feasibility quadrant

Risk Management Analysis

Table 6.2

Case Study 2: Transformation of Hospice Chain ABC Into an Automation-First Operation

Introduction: Hospice Chain ABC, a network of facilities providing end-of-life palliative care, is embarking on an organizational redesign and digital transformation journey to become an automation-first operation. With a focus on enhancing patient care, improving

Table 6.1 *Automation feasibility heatmap*

Process	Sales	Marketing	Inventory management	Finance	Human resources
Customer inquiries	Medium				
Order processing	High				
Sales reporting	Low				
Targeted marketing		High			
Campaign analysis		Medium			
Social media management		Low			
Stock replenishment			High		
Inventory tracking			High		
Supplier management			Medium		
Invoicing				High	
Expense management				Medium	
Financial reporting				Medium	
Recruitment					Medium
Training and development					Medium
Payroll administration					High
Employee onboarding					High

Table 6.2 Risk management analysis

Risk	Likelihood	Impact	Effort	Mitigation
Data breaches could result in reputational damage and legal liabilities.	M	H	M	Implement robust data governance and security measures. Conduct regular audits and ensure compliance with regulations.
Inadequate data infrastructure could impede the organization's ability to leverage customer data for strategic decision making, personalized marketing, and competitive advantage.	M	H	H	Invest in upgrading data infrastructure to support automation initiatives. Implement data governance policies to ensure data quality, security, and compliance with privacy regulations. .
Implementation may disrupt workflows and processes.	M	M	M	Conduct thorough impact assessments. Implement solutions gradually. Provide hypercare operational support.
Existing systems may not be compatible with new technologies.	M	H	H	Assess existing systems to identify options including upgrades or decommission. Develop integration plan, consider middleware solutions, research alternative solutions.

operational efficiency, and optimizing resource allocation, the organization seeks to leverage AI and automation throughout its operations.

The following are the results of their organizational assessments utilizing the McKinsey 7S Model, PESTLE analysis, gap analysis, and use case analysis.

McKinsey 7S

Strategy

Current state: currently, ABC's strategy primarily focuses on delivering palliative care to patients, with limited integration of automation technologies. While the organization strives to provide compassionate care, operational processes lack a standard approach, resulting in inefficiencies, resourcing challenges, and staff who are under pressure.

Desired state: in the future, ABC's strategy needs to evolve to prioritize patient-centric care while leveraging automation to enhance operational efficiency and resource allocation. This includes developing tailored care plans for patients using AI-driven predictive analytics and optimizing administrative processes through robotic process automation (RPA). The long-term strategy will emphasize continuous improvement and innovation to adapt to evolving patient needs and technological advancements in health care.

Structure

Current state: ABC's structure is hierarchical with multiple regional policies and limited cross-functional collaboration. Decision-making processes are centralized with delays resulting from the need for leadership approval.

Desired state: the desired structure will facilitate cross-functional collaboration and agility, enabling effective implementation of automation initiatives. This may involve creating interdisciplinary teams comprising health care professionals, IT specialists, and automation experts to drive automation projects. Adopting a matrix organizational structure will promote flexibility and responsiveness to change.

Systems

Current state: ABC's current health care systems lack integration and use many aging legacy systems. Existing systems do not have the capacity to utilize AI algorithms for personalized treatment recommendations. Data are currently stored in many different systems with no integration into a central source.

Desired state: the organization will modernize its health care systems to support automation technologies and deliver personalized patient care. This involves investing in electronic health record systems integrated with AI algorithms for real-time patient monitoring and treatment recommendations.

Shared Values

Current state: ABC's values prioritize compassionate care for patients and their families, but there is limited emphasis on innovation and continuous improvement and ways of working have not evolved for some time.

Desired state: the organization's values will reflect a commitment to compassionate, dignified care for patients and their families, coupled with a dedication to innovation and continuous improvement. Emphasizing patient comfort and well-being while embracing automation technologies will ensure that automation complements the human touch in end-of-life care.

Style

Current state: leadership at ABC lacks an appetite for transformation, and there is little expertise among board members on cognitive technology. Limited communication and collaboration between leadership and frontline staff impedes the integration of automation technologies into patient care processes.

Desired state: Leadership will undergo executive coaching that facilitates a transformational style to inspire a culture of innovation, learning, and adaptability. Leaders will champion the integration of automation technologies into patient care processes while ensuring employees feel empowered to contribute ideas for improvement. Open communication and collaboration between leadership and frontline staff is essential for driving the automation agenda while maintaining a patient-centric focus.

Skills

Current state: employees at ABC do not have access to the necessary training and support to transition to an automation-first operation. Limited investment in training programs and ongoing support may hinder the successful integration of automation technologies into patient care processes.

Desired state: comprehensive training programs on automation technologies as well as patient care best practices, and ethical considerations in health care automation will be crucial. Providing ongoing support and mentorship opportunities can help health care professionals adapt to new roles and responsibilities resulting from automation implementation, ensuring a smooth transition and continued delivery of high-quality patient care.

Staff

Current state: ABC faces challenges in attracting and retaining talent with expertise in automation, data analytics, and digital transformation. Limited investment in professional development opportunities has meant staff are relying on traditional manual processes to deliver the required services.

Desired state: ABC will invest in recruitment strategies targeting individuals with expertise in health care informatics, AI, and process automation. Additionally, upskilling opportunities and investment in nursing teams will enable them to excel in the arena of personalized patient care. Offering competitive compensation packages, professional development opportunities, and a supportive work environment will help attract top talent who can deliver excellence in health care delivery.

PESTLE Analysis

- Political:
  - ABC must adhere to regulatory frameworks governing health care and automation technologies, ensuring compliance with

laws related to patient privacy, data security, and medical
ethics.

- Economic:
  - o Economic factors such as budget constraints or fluctuations
    in health care funding could influence ABC's ability to invest
    in automation infrastructure and training programs.
  - o Economic shifts and market trends may affect patient
    demographics, health care demand, and reimbursement
    models, potentially influencing the prioritization and
    implementation of automation initiatives.
- Social:
  - o Changing demographics, such as an aging population, may
    drive demand for end-of-life care services.
  - o Social trends and patient expectations regarding technology-
    enabled health care may shape ABC's approach to the speed
    at which automation solutions should be implemented to
    enhance patient experiences.
- Technological:
  - o ABC must consider compatibility issues and integration
    challenges when adopting new automation technologies,
    ensuring seamless interoperability with external health care
    IT systems and infrastructure.
- Legal:
  - o ABC must adhere to legal requirements and health care
    regulations governing data privacy, patient confidentiality,
    and medical practice standards.
  - o Legal considerations regarding liability, malpractice, and risk
    management should be considered when deciding ABC's
    approach to implementing AI with a focus on mitigating
    potential legal risks.
- Environmental:
  - o ABC needs to consider environmental factors such as energy
    consumption, waste management, and sustainable practices,
    aligning with broader sustainability goals and corporate

social responsibility initiatives. This area could be made a priority for automation initiatives to drive efficiencies.

- o Environmental factors such as climate change and natural disasters may impact health care delivery and infrastructure resilience, meaning ABC needs to incorporate contingency plans and disaster preparedness measures into its automation strategy.

Gap Analysis

1. Technology integration:
   - Current state: ABC relies on traditional paper-based processes and legacy IT systems for patient management and administrative tasks.
   - Desired state: implementing automation technologies such as RPA and AI requires integrating disparate systems and transitioning to digital workflows.
   - Gap: the organization faces a significant gap in technology integration and readiness for automation, necessitating investments in IT infrastructure and digital products.
2. Staff training and adoption:
   - Current state: health care professionals and staff members do not have the necessary training and expertise to effectively utilize and adopt automation technologies.
   - Desired state: specialist employees should be skilled in automation tools and digital workflows.
   - Gap: the organization needs to bridge the gap in staff training and adoption by recruiting existing experts and providing comprehensive education and resources for health care automation.
3. Data management and security:
   - Current state: ABC manages sensitive patient data but lacks the necessary data infrastructure and security measures to support automation initiatives.

- Desired state: implementing AI and intelligent automation requires robust data management practices and compliance with health care privacy regulations.
- Gap: there is a gap in data management and security, requiring the organization to invest in data governance frameworks and cybersecurity measures to protect patient information.

4. Change management and culture:
   - Current state: while there is a commitment to innovation, there may be resistance to change among some health care professionals and staff members.
   - Desired state: enthusiasm and acceptance of technological advances that enhance people's ability to provide quality patient care driven by continuous improvement initiatives.
   - Gap: the organization needs to address resistance to change through effective change management strategies, advertising a human-centric commitment, and leadership support.

High-Level Impact Analysis for Automation Use Cases

Robotic Process Automation (RPA)

Use Case 1: automating administrative tasks such as patient admissions, discharge processes, and billing documentation.

Impact: RPA can significantly reduce manual errors, streamline workflows, and improve efficiency in administrative processes, allowing health care professionals the time to focus more on patient care.

Use Case 2: implementing automated medication adherence monitoring systems with reminders and alerts for patients and caregivers.

Impact: automated medication adherence systems can help ensure patients take their medications as prescribed, reducing the risk of medication errors, missed doses, and adverse drug reactions. By promoting medication adherence, these systems can improve symptom management, treatment effectiveness, and overall patient outcomes.

Artificial Intelligence (AI)

Use Case 1: implementing AI-driven analytics for symptom diagnosis and treatment planning based on patient data and medical histories.

Impact: AI can enhance clinical decision making, personalize treatment plans, and improve patient outcomes by proactively diagnosing symptoms and complications.

Use Case 2: deploying smart bedside monitoring systems equipped with sensors and AI algorithms to continuously monitor patients' vital signs, activity levels, and symptoms.

Impact: smart bedside monitoring systems can detect changes in patients' health status in real-time, alerting health care providers to potential issues or deteriorations. This proactive monitoring can lead to early interventions, improved symptom management, and enhanced patient safety and comfort.

Document Processing and Natural Language Processing (NLP)

Use Case 1: implementing intelligent document processing (IDP) to extract information from clinical notes, physician orders, and patient records. NLP can be used to summarize, analyze, and identify key recommendations to be reviewed by health care professionals.

Impact: IDP and NLP can automate the process of documentation, saving health care professionals time and reducing the risk of errors in medical records. It can also facilitate data analysis for research purposes and improve the accuracy of coding and billing.

Use Case 2: implementing IDP to efficiently manage end-of-life care directives and legal documents for patients and their families. NLP can be utilized to extract key information from legal documents, such as advanced directives and living wills, to ensure compliance with patient preferences and legal requirements.

Impact: IDP and NLP can streamline the management of legal documents related to end-of-life care, ensuring that patient preferences are accurately documented and digitally accessible to ABC nursing teams. This can enhance communication and decision making among patients, families, and care providers, improving the quality of care delivered during this sensitive time.

Machine Learning

Use Case 1: implementing machine learning algorithms to predict patients' risk of symptom exacerbation or acute events, such as pain crises or respiratory distress.

Impact: by leveraging machine learning, ABC can proactively identify patients at higher risk of deteriorating health and intervene pre-emptively to manage symptoms and prevent crises. This approach can improve patient comfort, reduce emergency hospital admissions, and enhance the overall quality of care in the hospice.

Use Case 2: employing machine learning algorithms to optimize resource scheduling and staffing levels based on patient needs, historical utilization patterns, and predicted demand.

Impact: by leveraging machine learning for resource scheduling, ABC can ensure that staffing levels align with patient demand, minimizing underutilization, or overstaffing scenarios. This should lead to more efficient use of resources, reduced administrative burden on staff, and improved overall operational efficiency in the hospice setting.

By leveraging a toolkit of different assessment techniques, organizations can gain a deeper understanding of their current state, identify areas for improvement, and develop targeted strategies to drive automation transformation. However, you should recognize that each approach has its limitations and may require customization to suit specific organizational contexts.

The key lies in selecting and adapting the most relevant elements from these models to create a tailored approach that addresses the unique challenges and opportunities faced by your organization. Through thoughtful analysis, strategic planning, and collaborative execution, we can navigate the complexities of transformation and realize our vision for the future.

CHAPTER 7

Blueprint for Creating the Intelligent Organization

I mentioned back in Chapter 2, how two versions of a roadmap will come in handy. We want a technical version with dates, dependencies, and ownership to form part of your detailed project management plan, and this will be the version that our team works toward and follows.

But we also need a visually engaging version for the purpose of communicating the big picture to your stakeholders and employees. Using storytelling techniques, branding, visual marketing, or humanizing your new digital co-workers are all options you can consider.

A high-level version with approximate dates should be enough to ensure the workforce is informed of how quickly they are likely to see changes. This might include stops on the roadmap such as:

1. **Enablement** (communications, change management, and training);
2. **Exploration** (organizational assessment, use case identification, and pipeline planning);
3. **Execution** (build, test, and deploy solutions);
4. **Enhancement** (enhance employee experience, continuous improvement, and data analytics) (Figure 7.1).

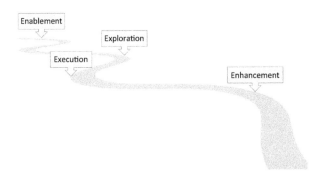

Figure 7.1 *Hyperautomation roadmap*

I love a bit of alliteration for memorability.

Let's go into more detail though, so you, the reader, can use this and the recommendations in this book to transform your organization.

In the spirit of storytelling, let me introduce you to our robot friend, Synthia, who has some missions for you to complete to enable automation and AI to transform your organization.

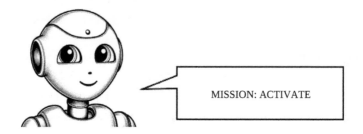

MISSION: ACTIVATE

1. **Leadership and project sponsor:**
   - Secure commitment from leadership to drive AI and automation initiatives.
   - Appoint a dedicated project sponsor to champion the transformation journey.
   - Develop a compelling business case highlighting the potential return on investment (ROI) and strategic advantages of AI and automation adoption.
   - Implement risk assessment and mitigation strategies to address potential barriers to implementation.
2. **Vision:**
   - Develop a clear vision outlining how AI and automation will drive business success.
   - Align the vision with organizational goals and values to inspire all stakeholders.
3. **Change and communication:**
   - Identify and engage key stakeholders to support the mission.
   - Implement effective change management strategies to ensure smooth adoption.

- Create audience-specific messaging to communicate the vision, benefits, and objectives of AI and automation initiatives across the organization.

MISSION: ASSEMBLE

4. **Automation team:**
   - Assemble a cross-functional team with expertise in AI,automation, change and improvement, and relevant businessdomains.
   - Ensure diverse perspectives and skills to drive innovation and problem-solving with a mix of internal and external talent.
5. **Governance council:**
   - Establish a governance council to oversee AI and automation initiatives.
   - Define policies, standards, and guidelines to ensure alignment with organizational objectives.
   - Agree and document the project methodology for delivering each intelligent automation solution.

MISSION: POWER UP

6. **Data strategy:**
   - Develop a comprehensive data visualization and analytics strategy to enable informed decision making and AI-driven insights.
   - Integrate a framework emphasizing data security, data quality, and data governance.
   - Establish reporting metrics for the transformation program benefits.

7. **Digital infrastructure:**
   - Build robust digital infrastructure to support AI and automation deployment.
   - Invest in scalable and secure cloud-based platforms and technologies.

8. **Tech stack:**
   - Evaluate, select, and install AI and automation software aligned with organizational goals.
   - Consider partnering with intelligent automation deployment specialists.
   - Install technology to facilitate improved ways of working for humans such as communication and collaboration software.

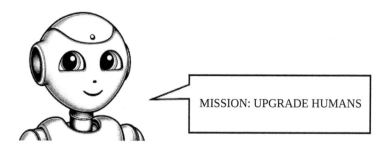

9. **Training and upskilling:**
   - Provide personalized training and mentoring programs to upskill and certify the core program employees with AI and automation skills.
   - Create a culture of continuous learning and development to adapt to evolving technologies.

10. **Role mapping and augmentation:**
   - Redefine roles and responsibilities to accommodate AI and automation integration.
   - Ensure clarity and alignment between humans and AI to maximize efficiency.
   - Restructure teams to integrate collaboration between humans and AI and facilitate cross-functional teamwork.

11. **Education and engagement:**
   - Implement change readiness and adoption strategies to support employees in transitioning to new ways of working with AI and automation.
   - Integrate mechanisms for managing change resistance and addressing concerns about job displacement or automation anxiety.
   - Develop education and engagement playbooks that promote AI and automation awareness and signpost how to submit ideas to the pipeline.
   - Establish citizen developer programs for scaling automation.
   - Encourage a spirit of exploration and experimentation, where bold ideas are encouraged and incentivized.

MISSION: INITIATE SCAN

12. **Assess organization and processes:**
   - Conduct a comprehensive organizational assessment to assess operational readiness and identify AI and automation use cases.
   - Analyze existing processes and workflows to uncover opportunities for automation.

13. **Gather and analyze data intelligence:**
   - Collect and analyze data intelligence to inform AI and automation strategies.
   - Identify patterns, trends, and insights to drive informed decision making.
   - Establish key metrics and success criteria for proposed use cases.

MISSION: OPTIMISE

14. **Redesign processes:**
   - Redesign processes to focus on outcome-driven transformational change as well as facilitating seamless collaboration between humans and AI.
   - Define clear roles and responsibilities for human-AI interaction and collaboration.
   - Match the redesigned processes to the appropriate intelligent automation technology.

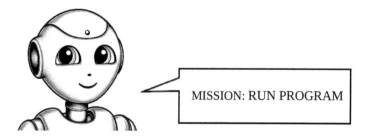

MISSION: RUN PROGRAM

15. **Build:**
   - Build AI and automation solutions based on identified use cases and requirements.

16. **Test:**
    - Conduct robust and thorough testing to validate the functionality and performance of AI and automation systems.
    - Solicit feedback from end-users to identify operational readiness or areas for improvement.

17. **Deploy:**
    - Roll out AI and automation initiatives in a phased manner, starting with pilot projects.
    - Manage the communications and business readiness for the go-live of the solutions

18. **Measure:**
    - Measure and monitor the performance, impact, and effectiveness of AI and automation initiatives.

19. **Improve:**
    - Continuously iterate and improve AI and automation solutions based on feedback and data insights.

MISSION: USER EXPERIENCE

20. **Improve employee experience:**
    - Leverage AI and automation benefits to streamline workflows and enhance employee satisfaction.
    - Utilize productivity efficiencies to implement employee-centric initiatives that promote well-being and work–life balance.

21. **Improve customer experience:**
    - Enhance customer interactions and services through AI-driven personalization and automation.
    - Deliver seamless and intuitive experiences across all touchpoints using both humans and AI to drive customer loyalty.

22. **Pursue ethical and sustainable AI practices:**
    - Utilize AI and automation to optimize resources, sustainability, and reduce environmental impact.
    - Implement initiatives to use AI for good and to support your corporate social responsibility goals.

MISSION: FUTURE-PROOFING

23. **Drive innovation, change, and improvement:**
    - Drive a culture of innovation and continuous improvement to continue transformation.
    - Encourage experimentation and collaboration to explore new possibilities with AI and automation.

24. **Embrace evolving and emerging technologies:**
    - Stay abreast of emerging technologies and trends to remain competitive and innovative.
    - Invest in research and development to explore new opportunities for AI and automation integration.
    - Establish collaboration pacts with industry partners and academia to stay at the forefront of technological innovation.

25. **Celebrate human and AI harmonization:**
    - Recognize and celebrate the successful integration of AI and automation into organizational processes.
    - Communicate successes to inspire confidence and engagement across the organization.
    - Continue to update your vision and roadmap for the next ambitious steps.
    - Recommend this book to your non-robot friends.

The high-level roadmap of enablement, exploration, execution, and enhancement provides a clear path forward to ensure clarity; this regular communication should help to eliminate anxiety about the program for the wider organization. The more detailed blueprint we've provided gives an ambitious plan for the key players in your transformation team, which lets them know what we're aiming for, as well as being suitable as a starting point for building your project plan.

Synthia wishes you good luck with your missions!

Selecting Your Technology

When embarking on your intelligent automation journey to radically redesign your organization, one of the most critical steps is selecting the right technology.

For generative AI, consider offerings such as OpenAI (ChatGPT) for text and image generation; Gemini 2 for text, images, and video; or Microsoft Copilot (which utilizes OpenAI's learning model integrated with Microsoft's own proprietary language model and real-time internet research via their Bing search capabilities.)[1]. For generative AI for just images, there is OpenAI's DALL-E 3, Google's ImageFX, Midjourney, or Adobe Firefly. For videos, at the time of writing, there are a large number of players beginning to open up the market, notably Colossyan and Synthesia. For audio only, think of providers such as WellSaid, Eleven Labs, or Speechify. For music, there's OpenAI's Jukebox, AIVA, or Splash PRO. And finally, for generating computer programming code, you could utilize GitHub Copilot or OpenAI's Codex.

It's important to note that since AI has become more open-source, and yes, a trendy buzzword (hey, I'm guilty too, I've written a book on it after all), there are more providers coming out all the time and the named companies are the first I thought of in that space, but by no means an exhaustive list or an endorsement. As always, do your research to select the most appropriate tool for your business and security needs. I'd suggest a technology and business needs analysis. This will provide you with the requirements that these technology vendors need to meet to satisfy your organizational needs and align to your vision of the art of the possible.

There are also options to use AI and machine learning developers to build your own large language model (LLM) for more specific needs. Or you could opt for private/enterprise models from these providers to ensure the output you generate is not shared past your firewalls and cannot be used for future training of the AI, this need will depend on your concerns over your intellectual property, regulations on data, or on your unique organization's requirements and resources.

For more advanced intelligent automation packages (think Robotic Process Automation (RPA), Machine Learning (ML), process mining, etc.), there are numerous providers in the market, each with their unique strengths and offerings. Some of the leading providers include Microsoft Power Automate, SS&C Blue Prism, UI Path, Automation Anywhere, and SAP Joule or SAP Process Automation, among others. It's essential to understand the capabilities of each provider and how well they align with your organization's needs.

Sending out a request for proposal (RFP) to automation vendors is a recommended step in assessing and evaluating potential technologies against your organization's vision and objectives. This due diligence helps you gather detailed information about each vendor's offerings and how they can support your goals.

- Consider the tech stack and product offering of each vendor. Ensure that the technology you choose can seamlessly integrate with your existing systems and processes, be suitable for your identified use cases, and should also be compatible with your future tech plans.
- Assess the scalability and future roadmap of the vendor. The chosen technology should be able to grow with your organization and adapt to future needs. The vendor's future roadmap can give you insights into their long-term plans and how they align with your growth strategy.
- Ensure that the vendor provides robust technical product and customer service support to address any issues and assist with user training and adoption. An active user community can also be extremely helpful in upskilling and evolving the skills and ideas in your team.
- Evaluate the user interface and experience of the technology to ensure it is intuitive and user-friendly with a view to being suitable for your team's capability and ambitions. The more

an application is no-code/low-code or has a simpler interface, or has a quick learning journey—then the easier it would be for business users, non-developers, to pick it up if you are considering citizen developers.

- Look for vendors that offer comprehensive implementation support, such as project delivery partnerships, professional services, and customer success support. These services can help ensure a successful implementation while you are still building your team's expertise and capability.
- Finally, consider the costs and compare the total cost of ownership of each technology. This includes not just the upfront costs, but also ongoing maintenance, support, and upgrade costs.

By carefully considering these points, you can select the technology that best fits your needs and supports your vision of radical redesign. Remember, the goal is not just to automate individual processes, but to transform your organization into a more efficient, innovative, and future-ready entity.

Building Your Infrastructure

Am I allowed to say: here comes the boring bit? CEOs look away now, we know you don't do the detail (OK, some of you do), but you can pass this section to your wonderful solution architects and infrastructure analysts.

We're going to get a bit technical, but we're not going to explain every term here, that's a different book. Which, while necessary, won't be as exciting as this one. I'm all about the creative, transformative possibilities of AI and automation, but I know that wouldn't be possible without getting this important stuff right.

When setting up your infrastructure for intelligent automation deployment, it's essential to get your experts to consider scalability, reliability, security, and performance. Here're some high-level notes that I've heard from my more technical friends on building a robust infrastructure:

- Utilize cloud platforms like AWS or Azure for computing resources, storage, and services, offering scalability, flexibility, and on-demand access.
- Consider deploying automation infrastructure across multiple cloud providers or using a hybrid approach for flexibility and resilience.
- Implement effective data management practices, including governance, quality assurance, and security measures.
- Prioritize security with encryption, access controls, and regular audits.
- Design an architecture supporting seamless integration with existing systems and application programming interfaces (APIs).
- Optimize performance and traffic management using data logging policies, caching, and load balancing.
- Implement monitoring and logging for performance, health, and security tracking.
- Conduct thorough performance testing of your infrastructure to identify bottlenecks, optimize resource allocation, and fine-tune system configurations for optimal performance.

Ok, technical stuff done, let's get back to imagining what's possible for our redesign.

Hyperautomation Project Delivery

Becoming automation-first is our transformational program, but each solution you build should be treated as a mini project. It doesn't matter what methodology you use, PRINCE2, agile sprints, waterfall, kanban, six sigma to name a few. You just need to ensure you deliver each project in a consistent and replicable manner to accelerate your time to deliver and improve each time. The key is to use the approach that fits your organization and the project's specific needs and objectives.

In this diagram, I'm not offering anything new or groundbreaking, but it serves to remind us that people are at the core of all we do. Processes should be assessed and redesigned as a cyclical activity before we add the technology. Similar to what we build, as can be seen on the right, we design the solution based on our re-engineered process then build, test, and deploy. Importantly for hyperautomation, we improve on all we do, by embracing innovation (Figure 7.2).

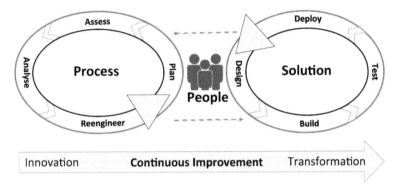

Figure 7.2 Hyperautomation delivery methodology

Scaling and Evolving Intelligent Automation

Once the proof of concept is completed, the initial implementation is done, and the first automation and AI use cases are fully embedded and providing benefits, the next step is to scale and evolve intelligent automation across the wider organization.

Here are some tips on how to do this.

Standardization and Reusability

- Standardization is pivotal in scaling efficiently. By establishing standardized processes, organizations can ensure consistency and streamline operations across departments. Process mining then becomes more useful to identify adherence or variation from standardized, agreed process execution, or in identifying further opportunities for streamlining.
- Utilize a standardized project delivery methodology to ensure automation projects are delivered consistently using the same framework each time.

- Use templates for standardizing and reusing documentation for consistency and ease of use.
- For each automation you build, consider how components can be reused by different departments in the future, perhaps those who use the same system for different processes. For example, for each business application, provide a template for automating the login and menu navigation screen—enabling the next automation build to quickly utilize this and not duplicate build work.[2]
- Develop a template library of anything that can be utilized or copied (documentation, AI prompts, and automation flows) to reduce the time and resources required for subsequent projects. This approach not only accelerates the deployment but also enables consistency and professional standards.

Citizen Developer Programs

- Empower nontechnical employees from the business to build their own automations. Citizen developer programs are becoming more popular and are influencing the user interface and training programs that automation providers offer, leaning more frequently toward providing low-code and no-code applications, with still the potential for more advanced coding and customization. In my experience, they can really unleash a wave of innovation, enhance change acceptance, and enable automation to spread quickly among volunteers and early adopters throughout the entire organization.
- Keep these programs open to any volunteers and provide the employees with the tools, training, mentoring, and support needed to create their own automation solutions. Carefully define the scope for what citizen developers can automate; ideally, simple linear processes, non-cross-functional processes related to their own department or tasks, and automations that can utilize our library templates.
- Establish a structured review process from the center of excellence (CoE) or Governance Council to ensure

consistency, quality, and alignment with organizational objectives. I recommend a framework that I call the **4As: assess, accept, advise, and approve.**

Assess

- Evaluate the proposed automation initiative to determine its feasibility, alignment with organizational goals, and potential impact on business processes.
- Assess the technical requirements, resource availability, reusability potential, and estimated support or mentoring needs.

Accept

- Confirm that the initiative addresses a genuine business need and offers tangible benefits such as improved efficiency, cost savings, or enhanced customer experience.
- Assign a mentor and any reusable templates for the solution.
- Acceptance signifies endorsement of the initiative to proceed to the next stage of development and implementation.

Advise

- Provide constructive feedback and guidance to the citizen developer on the solution build and design.
- Support with testing and offer recommendations for optimizing the proposed solution, addressing any identified gaps or areas for improvement.
- Share best practices, lessons learned, and relevant resources to support the successful execution of the initiative.

Approve

- Grant formal approval for the automation initiative to be deployed to live.

- Ensure that all necessary resources, support, test results, documentation, and approvals are in place to facilitate the execution and initial monitoring.
- Measure the success of these initiatives as part of your overall reporting on the benefits.
- Celebrate and publicly reward and recognize the shining examples of the work done by citizen developers to spark curiosity and ideas among other employees.

By leveraging the business expertise of employees across various departments, organizations can rapidly identify and automate manual processes, scaling the usage of automation beyond your centrally led project.

Automation as a Service

Implementing automation as a service introduces a structured approach to automation deployment and management. By offering automation services as a centralized resource, departments can access and utilize automation capabilities on-demand. Introducing cross-charging mechanisms incentivizes departments to leverage automation solutions and drives widespread adoption while ensuring the cost-effectiveness of automation initiatives.

Continuous Improvement

Regularly reviewing and refining automation processes ensures that they remain aligned with organizational goals and evolving business needs. By soliciting feedback from end-users and stakeholders, we can identify areas for enhancement and implement iterative improvements to maximize the value derived from our investment in the technology.

Center of Excellence (CoE)

Establishing a CoE will provide the governance, knowledge sharing, standards, and best practices needed for an automation rollout. Centralizing intelligent automation expertise can accelerate the implementation and adoption of automation solutions and ensure consistency and quality across projects. However, it's important not to rely solely on your CoE for building solutions. As demand grows, consider deploying developers across other business functions or engaging citizen developers. This approach allows for the concurrent creation of multiple solutions, with the CoE providing expertise for escalation, governance, and reporting.

Maintaining a Healthy Pipeline

Sustaining a pipeline of potential projects will ensure continued success. Organizations should continuously evaluate and prioritize processes ripe for automation, considering factors such as complexity, impact, and strategic alignment. The use of process mining, pipeline submission incentives, and employee awareness campaigns can help to continue to generate further opportunities. By maintaining a pipeline, organizations can sustain momentum and keep the project going past your original proof of concept.

Where there're manual, electronic, and rules-based processes still being executed by humans, you still have more you can do to free up your people.

Cloud-Based Infrastructure

Embracing cloud-based infrastructure offers scalability, flexibility, and cost-effectiveness for automation initiatives. Cloud platforms give you the agility to rapidly deploy and scale automation solutions while minimizing infrastructure overheads.

AI-Driven Workforce Planning

Utilize AI scheduling tools to review the performance, activities, and schedules of your AI and human colleagues. Focus on maximizing the efficiency and effectiveness via methods such as 24/7 operations (your robots don't need a break), sharing capacity among multiple business divisions, reporting to monitor trends or exceptions, considering seasonal peaks and demands, or workload monitoring to respond to bottlenecks or excess demand, to ensure optimal performance and productivity.[3]

Some organizations automate their automation, using orchestration tools to ensure the robots are allocated automatically to process the highest priority work first in accordance with your service level agreements.[4]

Continually assess the ROI of your program. For example, you may have an RPA job that has been running for several years but no longer has many cases to work. It may be better to assign that sporadic and less frequent task back to your people, allowing that digital resource to be reassigned to more high-priority and cost-effective work. Also, really question when approaching a potential new automation, change to existing automation or update: "Is this worth the cost and time of doing this work?" This is something that needs to be balanced and measured against the business impact. You are here to be as efficient as the tools you're using after all.

Lastly, consider the collaboration and integration between AI and human workers to improve "human-in-the-loop" decision making and smooth, responsive handovers to harness the full potential of your combined workforce.

Successful Implementation Case Studies

Let's have a look at some companies that have implemented AI and automation and why I think they were a success.

1. The global brewery organization, Heineken, partnered with automation provider UiPath to automate 140 processes which save them 14,000 hours every month. Starting with their finance team, they created a "a thirst for automation" and evolved into a hyperautomation model. They utilized intelligent automation, document processing, low-code development, chatbot development, toolchains, test automation, and digital integration in

their tech stack. They used an agile delivery methodology of continuous improvement and constant collaboration.

Starting with a vision that "Automation will help people in their jobs. It will free up time to focus on value-added activities and being creative," they structured their approach of a central hyperautomation team for governance and localized teams who worked semiautonomously. The hyperautomation team had a brand and a centralized hub of knowledge and created education and awareness through workshops, technical courses, build-a-bot sessions, and sharing successes.

One aspect I really like is how they humanized their robot with each having a persona and CV detailing, "When it was born, what it does, the value it brings, how often it works, who manages it, if it's reducing errors, speeding up tasks, or saving hours."[5]

2. Heathrow Airport looked to automation after having downsized its IT operations during the pandemic. Automation became a key strategy to empower all employees, not just IT, to utilize no-code or low-code automation tools to deliver productivity and innovation. Building a community of employees who were empowered to utilize these automation tools and tailor the automations they built to their specific goals and departments, they evolved the practice using communication of the benefits, IT guidance, education on the technology, and a community that shared support and resources.

Educate people on the benefits of automation, put the right tools in their hands, and trust them to build what is needed and most impactful. This approach means we should see less of a fear of automation, and instead an increase in employee engagement as employees can autonomously elect to automate the parts they feel need it the most, leaving them in control still. "We created a community that empowers employees to spot and deliver digital opportunities, but also equips them to avoid duplication, reduce manual processes, improve productivity and enhance our overall digital experience."[6]

3. In West Yorkshire in the United Kingdom, Calderdale Council transformed its operations with intelligent automation, AI, and NLP. The case study described in *The Autonomous Enterprise: Powered by AI* outlines several factors that were key to success. They integrated automation as part of a broader digital project that also included enhancing their customer-facing website, with strong executive support providing a vision for the project of improving their digital services and increasing customer satisfaction. They kept the end customer experience in mind by using intelligent virtual assistants to respond to customer requests, while also ensuring real-person support remained available.

   Internally, an automation team drove initiatives and implementation forward, but with responsibility devolved to business teams to own automation efforts, creating that collaboration between humans and robots in all teams for maximum efficiency.

   Effective communication with stakeholders was highlighted as important and continuous improvement was embraced, with customer surveys and automation and business teams feedback loops to refine automated processes.

   Calderdale Council optimized processes, enhanced service, and achieved efficiency gains, but what stands out to me most was the power of collaboration between people and intelligent automation when prioritizing strong customer focus.

4. Equinix, a global provider in digital infrastructure, implemented RPA software to revolutionize its operations, streamline processes and free up its employees for more value-added activities. Their program improved data accuracy, accelerated vendor

payments, saved seven million dollars in operating costs, and freed up approximately 175,000 employee hours.

Impressive! But what I want to highlight as role models to emulate is what they did with those hours saved, and their commitment to employee empowerment and continuous learning. "In Equinix's 'digital accelerator community,' employees dedicate time to improving their skill sets and discovering new ways to contribute to the business. The company believes that continuous improvement is key to accelerating digital transformation."[8] Equinix did all the right things starting with a compelling vision of "Find a better way" as well as empowering citizen developers throughout the organization. The money saved via automation is invested back into employee experience improvements, as well as strategic initiatives, which results in an innovative, productive, and engaged workforce who will continue to use intelligent automation to find that better way.

CHAPTER 8

Process Re-Engineering for a Radical Redesign

One of my favorite catchphrases is that "nothing changes unless you make changes." This is useful in all aspects of life of course, but it's also why process re-engineering is vital in the approach to organizational redesign.

Process re-engineering is about giving your organization a much-needed makeover to the way it operates. Shaking things up and reshaping the way business processes work to make big improvements in how efficiently things get done, how effective they are, and how happy your customers are. Happy customers are loyal customers.

Instead of automating your processes as-is, or just adding AI prompts into an existing process, or altering small steps here and there such as with process improvement, instead process re-engineering means taking a step back and totally reimagining how things are done from the ground up.

So, what does that mean and how do we approach it?

Well, you need to start by **identifying processes** to re-engineer. These are typically core business processes that directly impact the organization's goals, performance, or customer and employee satisfaction.

Once these processes have been identified the next step is to **analyze the as-is process**. You conduct a thorough analysis to understand how these processes currently operate. This involves mapping out each step of the process, identifying bottlenecks, inefficiencies, waste, and areas for potential improvement.

Now it's time to **set objectives**. There must be clear objectives and goals established for the re-engineering intention. These objectives should be aligned with the organization's overall strategic goals and should focus on improving key performance metrics such as cost, quality, speed, and customer and employee satisfaction/sentiment.

We are ready to **re-engineer processes**. Based on the analysis of current processes and the established objectives, the processes are redrawn from a blank page with nothing off the table, considering your now combined workforce of humans and AI. The key is to think if you were starting from scratch today, with everything you know now, and the technology already in place,[1] what would this process look like? This involves challenging existing assumptions, removing unnecessary steps, simplifying complex steps or tasks, and integrating the right technology where appropriate. Think about the different skill sets of your human and digital co-workers, you have the opportunity here to do things faster, more efficiently or to add value-added steps that you didn't have the time or resource for before.

Change is good! We understand this but that doesn't necessarily mean the people impacted by the change will agree, any change made to their world without their input can cause resistance or challenge. So, we need to **involve stakeholders**. Stakeholder involvement is crucial throughout the re-engineering process. This includes employees at all levels of the organization, customers, suppliers, and other relevant stakeholders. Their knowledge on processes and the organization is not something you will be able to learn quickly so leverage their skills to your advantage. Their input and feedback help ensure that the re-engineered processes meet their needs and expectations, and mitigate that fear of change.

At this point, we should be good to go and **implement the changes**. Once the re-engineered processes are finalized and been through a period of piloting or testing, they are implemented across the organization. This may involve changes to organizational structure, job roles, workflows, technology systems, policies, and procedures. We mustn't forget that it is a necessity that our people receive **training and communication** critical to ensure that all employees understand the new processes and their roles within them. This may involve training programs, workshops, documentation, and ongoing support.

Once these changes have been rolled out it's important to understand the impact. That means you need to **monitor and measure performance**. Post the implementation, the performance of the re-engineered processes needs to be continuously monitored and measured against the established objectives. Key performance indicators (KPIs) are used to track progress and identify areas for further improvement. It is important that you keep that improvement ethos in place and don't make the mistake of thinking that making a change once means it's done, so if further efficiencies have been identified as part of the monitoring and measuring performance step, you need to move into **continuous improvement**. Process re-engineering is an ongoing effort. Continuous monitoring, feedback, and adaptation are essential to ensure that the redesigned processes remain effective and relevant in a changing business environment.

And lastly, don't forget to give yourself the pat on the back you deserve and some space to understand your learnings, now is when your final step kicks in: **celebrate success and learn from failures**. Successful implementation of re-engineered processes should be celebrated, and lessons learned from both successes and failures should be used to inform future re-engineering efforts.

Ok, hopefully, that brings you up to speed and takes care of "what is process re-engineering" and the steps needed, it's time to look at why we should approach it … the WIIFM (what's in it for me?).

If you're here and reading this book, it means you're aware your organization NEEDS change, it needs to move with ever-emerging trends, technologies, and employee needs. But there's more to it than these high-level motivations for change that process re-engineering brings to the table.

Process re-engineering is a powerhouse for radical redesign and you can reap the following benefits from it:

1. **Efficiency improvement:** Process re-engineering aims to streamline and optimize business processes to make them more efficient and effective. By eliminating waste, reducing redundant processes, and improving workflow, organizations can achieve

significant cost savings, enhance productivity, create a better customer and employee experience, therefore delivering faster results.

2. **Quality enhancement:** Re-engineering processes often involves standardizing procedures, implementing best practices, and incorporating quality control measures. This helps organizations deliver higher-quality products and services, meet customer expectations, improve overall satisfaction and sentiment.

3. **Customer focus:** Process re-engineering emphasizes the importance of aligning business processes with customer needs and expectations. By redesigning processes from the customer's perspective, organizations can enhance customer experience, increase loyalty, and gain a competitive edge in the market.

4. **Innovation and adaptability:** Re-engineering processes encourage innovation and agility by challenging existing assumptions, embracing new technologies, and exploring creative solutions to business challenges. This enables organizations to adapt to changing market conditions, seize opportunities, and stay ahead of the game.

5. **Risk management:** Re-engineering processes can help organizations identify and mitigate risks by improving transparency, accountability, and compliance.

6. **Organizational alignment:** Process re-engineering prompts organizational alignment by breaking down silos, empowering cross-functional collaboration, building on a shared understanding of goals and objectives. This helps create a unified and integrated organizational structure that is better equipped to achieve strategic objectives and better prepares them for organizational redesign, breaking down the stigma of approaching digital change.

7. **Change management:** Process re-engineering that uses effective change management to ensure successful implementation can enhance adoption of the new processes. By involving employees in the redesign process, providing training and support, and communicating the rationale and benefits of the changes,

organizations can minimize resistance and maximize employee buy-in.

There are so many examples of organizations that were not quick enough or willing enough to consider process re-engineering or innovation, which left them out in the cold when technology, culture, and external environmental factors changed. Such as back in Chapter 1, where we remembered Blockbuster, an organization that didn't adapt to the changes needed.

So, let's look at an example of an organization that reacted to the changes in the market and redesigned processes to ensure growth and continual operation. Blockbuster famously turned down the opportunity to buy Netflix and instead was surpassed by it; so, how did Netflix learn from Blockbuster's failure to move with the times and not let itself become extinct like its predecessor?

When Netflix was founded in 1997, it started as a DVD rental-by-mail service, disrupting the traditional video rental industry dominated by brick-and-mortar stores like Blockbuster. However, as technology evolved and consumer preferences shifted toward online, Netflix recognized the need to adapt its business model to stay relevant.

In 2007, Netflix launched its streaming service, allowing subscribers to instantly watch a wide range of TV shows and movies over the internet. This move marked a significant shift in the company's strategy, as it began to transition from a DVD rental company to a digital streaming platform.

But then Netflix reinvented itself again, and instead of just streaming content made by others, it shifted its business model to create its own. Netflix continued to invest heavily in content creation and licensing agreements, producing original series and movies to differentiate itself from competitors and attract subscribers. The company also embraced data analytics to personalize recommendations and improve the user experience.

As a result of these strategic initiatives, Netflix experienced exponential growth, expanding its subscriber base globally and becoming a dominant force in the entertainment industry. By re-engineering its business model and embracing digital innovation, Netflix successfully transformed itself from a DVD rental company into a leading streaming platform and content creator, disrupting the traditional media landscape in the process.[2]

Sadly, not everyone is as old as me to remember the delights of going to your local Blockbuster on a Friday night to pick up your films for the weekend, but there are very few households without Netflix, (other streaming services are also available!). That's because they made the Friday video rental an everyday occurrence and more accessible to their consumers. They also garnered loyalty and kept users on the platform by recommending new shows using machine learning algorithms based on our views and likes, we no longer needed to chat to the guy at the counter to see what other titles he would recommend, which also kept us on the platform for longer.

Now that we've explored what re-engineering is and why it's important, it's time to focus on the *how*. There are various techniques available to help you identify areas for re-engineering. he following are additional methods worth considering as you begin the process.

Process Mining

Process mining is a powerful analytical tool that harnesses data sourced from IT applications to reveal, monitor, and refine operational processes.

Process mining provides incredibly useful insights into how workflows operate, helping to identify bottlenecks, inefficiencies, and areas where improvements can be made. Essentially, it acts as a key driver for strategically redesigning processes, promoting greater operational flexibility and optimization.

Many organizations use process mining when they have exhausted their *low-hanging fruit* in change initiatives as it provides a different lens on where processes or parts of processes are still holding parts of the organization back. In some process improvement techniques, we rely on the people conducting the processes to provide all the relevant information to understand how to change the process. People have their own motivations or inabilities to not highlight all the changes required to make an impact or to gatekeep processes they don't want to change. This is why process mining can highlight the areas that may have been missed.

However, a very important caveat here is to be transparent regarding the use of process mining tools. If you want to win the hearts and minds of your employees, don't let them feel like *Big Brother* is watching them.

Value Stream Mapping

Value stream mapping helps you understand and enhance how materials and information move to deliver a product or service to customers. By carefully mapping each step from start to finish, businesses can spot where resources are wasted (Figure 8.1).

Using this method, they can identify inefficiencies and produce plans to make processes smoother, cut costs, reduce wait time, and boost productivity and customer happiness. That's why it's a great strategy for finding opportunities to re-engineer processes.

It also helps to promote the adoption of change. You need the experts in the process, your stakeholders, to be part of this activity. Their involvement is vital, making them part of creating the solution and therefore empowering them to build their new world.

Customer Analysis

Customer analysis gives useful perspectives that shape process improvement efforts by spotting challenges, understanding customer needs,

Figure 8.1 Value stream map example

segmenting customers for specific improvements, and predicting future demands.

By looking at customer feedback, complaints, and satisfaction surveys, businesses can highlight areas in the current process needing improvement. Understanding what customers prefer helps prioritize changes that directly tackle their concerns, boosting satisfaction and loyalty. Segmenting customers lets businesses tailor improvements to different groups, making the process more effective overall. Lastly, by analyzing past behavior to predict future needs, businesses can adjust their processes proactively, keeping up with evolving customer expectations and staying competitive in the long run.

Customer sentiment provides valuable insights on how to ensure they retain their relationship with you. This is why data insights provide you with the ability to change, to match and adapt to what they want and need from your business.

Customer Journey Mapping

Much like customer analysis, customer journey mapping helps businesses see the entire path customers take when they interact with a product or service. It shows where customers might run into problems or feel frustrated along the way. By looking at these touchpoints, businesses can figure out which parts of the process need fixing (Figure 8.2).

Customer journey maps also give insight into what customers want and how they feel at different stages of their journey. This understanding helps prioritize which areas to focus on for improvement. Plus, visually mapping out the journey makes it clear where things might be taking too long or where there's unnecessary repetition.

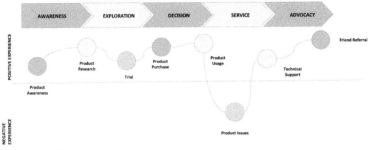

Figure 8.2 Customer journey map

By spotting these inefficiencies, businesses can re-engineer processes to make them smoother and more satisfying for customers.

Typically, customer journey mapping is used fairly early on in the process re-engineering process.

Root Cause Analysis

Root cause analysis is essential for process re-engineering because it helps teams dig deep and understand the real reasons behind process problems. Instead of just fixing surface-level issues, it allows them to find out what's truly causing inefficiencies or failures, whether it's outdated systems, workflow bottlenecks, or human errors. By tackling these root causes directly, teams can make changes that really make a difference, leading to smoother operations and better outcomes. It's like finding the main source of a problem rather than just dealing with its symptoms, which ultimately helps organizations work smarter and achieve long-term success.

A great exercise to help with root cause analysis is the Lean method —"the five whys." We want to re-engineer the process so our new technology can fix the root cause, not the problem statement (Figure 8.3).

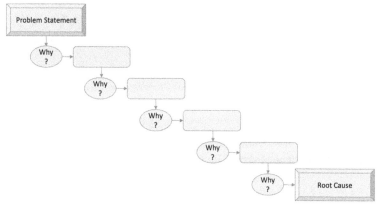

Figure 8.3 The five whys

Simulation and What-If Analysis

Simulation and what-if analysis is perfect for AI to enact process re-engineering, offering a glimpse into possible futures before committing to any major changes.

With simulation, different scenarios can be tested which allows exploration of alternative paths, much like mapping out different routes before a journey. This gauges the potential outcomes of adjustments and identifies the most promising avenues for improvement.

In essence, simulation and what-if analysis empowers organizations to drive a course of action that maximizes efficiency, minimizes risks, and leads to tangible changes in processes.

Simulation and what-if analysis are chosen over other methods in process re-engineering because they provide a comprehensive and risk-free way to experiment with different scenarios and evaluate their potential impacts before implementation. Unlike some other methods that may rely on trial and error or require actual changes to be made to the process, AI simulation allows for virtual testing without disrupting ongoing operations.

Predictive Analysis

In process re-engineering, predictive analysis uses historical data and patterns to foresee future outcomes. Through advanced algorithms and machine learning techniques, it detects potential obstacles or areas of concern in advance, allowing organizations to proactively address them.

Predictive analysis can be used once you have exhausted less complex techniques as this provides a deeper insight into organizational data allowing for forecasted outcomes, rather than something like trend analysis.

Data-Driven Decision Making

Much like predictive analysis, data-driven decision making powers process re-engineering by providing a solid core of factual insights and evidence. By interrogating data across various process variations—like performance metrics, resource usage, and customer input—organizations can grasp the full picture of current strengths, weaknesses, and areas for growth.

By consistently monitoring and evaluating process performance using data-driven metrics, organizations can fine-tune their re-engineering efforts over time, ensuring sustainable enhancements and better outcomes.

Ultimately, embracing data-driven decision making nurtures a culture of ongoing improvement, empowering organizations to adapt in an ever-changing landscape.

Digital Twin Simulation

Digital twin simulation transforms process re-engineering by offering a virtual sandbox for testing and refining systems in real time. Like creating a digital clone of processes, allowing experimentation with different scenarios, analyzing the outcomes, and spotting areas for improvement without any real-world consequences.

This is the big dress rehearsal before the show—allowing fine-tuning of strategies, figuring out what works best, and boosting performance. With this technology, smarter decisions can be made, and operations can be streamlined. Digital twin simulation provides the confidence to innovate, while ensuring that process re-engineering efforts lead to real, impactful improvements.

Digital twin simulation can be considered a more advanced approach to process re-engineering. While traditional process re-engineering methods focus on analyzing and redesigning existing processes based on historical data and observations, digital twin simulation takes it a step further by creating a virtual replica of the processes. This allows organizations to experiment with various scenarios, test out changes, and predict outcomes in a controlled environment before implementing them in the real world.

Your as-is processes were designed for humans, and may include wasteful or inefficient steps that your digital co-workers don't need to do, or can do in a different order, or can do simultaneously in seconds. We shouldn't assume the current process is the best way to do things, and that's why process re-engineering should be a core principle for you.

But it's about more than just making superficial changes; it's a strategic overhaul of how work gets done, aiming to streamline processes, cut unnecessary steps, and harness the latest technologies, in particular AI and automation, to boost performance.

By re-evaluating and redesigning core business processes, organizations can adapt to shifting market demands, technological advancements, and competitive landscapes. This means breaking away from the old and embracing the new, with a focus on innovation and improvement as your primary motivation. Emerging technologies are a huge enabler to keep the organization thriving and relevant for the future.

Process re-engineering nurtures a culture of continuous improvement and adaptability within organizations. It encourages teams to constantly seek out opportunities for optimization and experiment with new ideas. By adopting this mindset, organizations can stay agile and resilient when faced with challenges or market changes, ensuring they remain relevant and responsive to customer needs. Process re-engineering isn't just about making things run smoother today; it's essential for building a future-ready organization where human and AI collaboration thrives. By redesigning processes to fully integrate both, businesses can unlock innovation with a dynamic workforce that leverages the strengths of both people and technology. In doing so, they lay the foundation for long-term success in an ever-evolving digital landscape.

CHAPTER 9

Evolving Talent and Roles for the AI-Powered Workplace

The Role of HR and L&D

Human resources (HR) and learning and development (L&D) are needed as strategic architects, to build the redesign.

HR should own the change requirements for roles, policies, and employee experience. L&D should design and implement people development strategies that align with making hyperautomation a reality. This involves identifying key skills required to utilize cognitive computing and for other digital skills, creating targeted training programs, and establishing pathways for career progression.

This should be a collaborative effort, leveraging the expertise of HR in talent management and L&D in learning methodologies, so organizations can create a robust framework for developing a skilled and adaptable workforce.

The employee experience in an AI-powered workplace is shaped by HR practices that prioritize engagement, well-being, and career satisfaction. HR plays a crucial role in understanding the evolving needs of employees as we embrace the future of work and designing policies that support a positive and inclusive work environment.

Role Mapping

Role mapping should begin with your futuristic vision, incorporating AI to predict and design roles based on emerging technologies and business needs. The following exercise should be designed in collaboration with leadership and any senior leaders representing IT, and your intelligent automation projects. We need a complete redesign from a blank page with the roles and skills our future workforce needs, but do this exercise first without reference to the real people we have as we will map our people in at the end.

1. Begin with supporting functions that keep the business operating but don't directly execute the core business purpose or service, like HR, continuous improvement, or IT, for example.
2. List the critical roles required first.
3. Consider what existing roles are still required as we transition.
4. Indicate whether these existing roles will still be required once we are in the future state.
5. List the new roles we will require when AI is prevalent in the department.
6. List the existing roles that are no longer required.
7. Provide a simple, brief description for each role.
8. Include a list of the technical skills required, any essential* qualifications required (e.g., legal/medical/quality/regulatory) and any creative or soft skills that are imperative to delivering success. (*This should be essentials only, not desired. Stop asking for degrees please if experience at that skill is just as useful.)
9. Next, do the same exercise for the business functions that directly impact on your core business purpose, like warehousing and distribution, sales, customer service, laboratories, manufacturing, and so on.
10. Finally, consider roles in new departments that may be required, such as data science, user experience, and the automation center of excellence.
11. Once we have the roles required, you can group them into your chosen organizational structure, deciding if they are grouped by project, client, leader, business function, or other.
12. When you have your groups, list the roles of team managers or specialist leads or heads of business functions—if they tie in with your chosen structure from Chapter 2.

13. Next map how these groups should affect leadership structure and indicate which leadership roles need changing or if any new roles are required.

14. Only at this stage should we map our existing people against the roles we have identified.

15. Assess if the identified people meet the skillset required or if gaps are apparent.

16. Assess if those named in roles that are no longer required can be reskilled and transitioned into new roles or require consultation for redundancy. (Reskilling should be the priority.)

17. This provides us with an action plan for both L&D to make sure we have the right skills as well as HR for recruitment, role consultations, and talent retention.

18. Use this information to provide data for your change management teams so that impact analysis and risk management can be considered in the organizational change management plan (Table 9.1).

Talent Mapping

Talent mapping involves analyzing our people in their current roles, responsibilities, and skill sets, to map them against the organization's present and future needs. We need to identify high-potential individuals and highly skilled individuals, understand their career aspirations, and evaluate their capacity for growth, development, and their suitability for critical or future roles. When we understand what talent we have, and what skills our current people have, we can use this information to earmark people for the roles we have identified or for future development into these roles.

Use existing data from your HR systems such as performance and career goals to help with this activity. You should also consider skill assessments where each person would rate themselves, their peers, their teams, and their managers on their current skill level and desired skill development—the results of this would require calibration with key stakeholders across the business. It's also recommended that clear, reassuring communication is delivered around the purpose of a skills

Table 9.1 Role mapping

Role	Description	Grouping	Critical?	New?	Transition?	Not Required	Skills
Job title	Simplest explanation of purpose				P (permanent)/T (temporary)		Technical creative soft qualifications

assessment, that it's for future career development plans as well as succession planning.

Don't discount new ideas though, we are undergoing a radical redesign after all. Perhaps allow employees to tell you what other talents they have, rather than selecting from a predefined list related to their role. Maybe in their spare time, they are a whizz at programming or graphic design but don't get the opportunity to show this in their current role—we need to know this, especially if it's a talent they are wanting to use and especially if it's a skill we need in one of our roles.

Organizations often use the nine-box talent grid, (see figure 9.1), to rate both current performance and future potential. However, I would recommend you be primarily led by skills, rather than potential for promotion. For example, someone who maps as a "workhorse" but has machine learning skills, or even aspirations for this area, may be exactly who we need in that role. However, as we look for leaders, coaches, and advocates, the talent grid should give us exactly the people we want for future progression (Figure 9.1).

Talent and Performance Management

With roles, skills, and aspirations mapped, the next vital step is to nurture the workforce to be equipped for the future as we move into the era of hyperautomation. This requires investment into the growth of our people, ensuring they feel competent, satisfied, know their development plan, and feel comfortable with how they achieve the career growth needed to realize our vision. HR should create and own a talent management strategy that delivers this.

In-depth, one-on-one coaching sessions are recommended, not only for plotting growth but also to help with change management as we transition. Individual coaching should be offered so it can be meticulously tailored to the specific needs of individuals venturing into new or changing roles. These sessions can be delivered via specific coaching consultants, experienced HR or L&D folk, or perhaps even trained AI mentors.

Performance management conversations should take place not just in a formal review, but as part of an ongoing work culture that

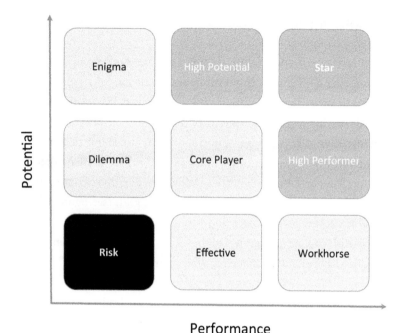

Potential

Performance

Figure 9.1 Talent grid

values continuous, two-way feedback. These conversations need to be identifying skill gaps and the employees' desire and capacity to resolve these gaps. We need to be collaboratively setting performance improvement goals and offering the training, mentoring, coaching, and time to bridge these gaps. We need to provide a high-challenge, high-support philosophy, where we can stretch our employees to be equipped for the future in a workplace that supports them to meet ambitious goals.

Cultivate a culture where employees actively participate in defining their growth aligned to our goals, and where managers or coaches create an environment where skill gaps are not only identified but promptly, supportively, and proactively addressed.

Recognizing the individual needs of each employee's career, we should collaboratively craft highly individualized career development plans covering strengths, interests, and long-term career aspirations. It should be clear to management, or coaches, whether employees are satisfied with their career level and with their role grouping or business function. Find out if they desire to progress, and if they do, what skill gaps exist that need to be addressed to enable this. For employees, they should be clear on the future of their role, and how automation may affect what the role entails. Employees need to have a clear and realistic plan of how they need to progress both with technical skills and for soft skills, and for any aspirational goals they have, how, and if, we can support them with realizing this.

Current performance needs to be a focus for development plans too. If there are concerns about meeting objectives or performance in their existing role, then clear guidelines and expectations need to be communicated with how we can support them and what specific measurements they need to improve, and how. Consistent low-performers at all levels of the organization do need to be dealt with though, if development and performance improvement haven't worked then we need to compassionately support them to exit the business. If we can't change people, then we change our people; our future needs people who will strive with us to hit our goals.

This will also feed into our succession planning strategy, identifying, and nurturing future leaders, to ensure a seamless transition and continuity in critical roles.

Talent Retention

Integral to our redesign is then making sure we retain that talent we have carefully identified and mapped to roles. This means the workplace must be one in which they feel valued, satisfied, rewarded, and that they have purpose.

This means monetary incentives, clear communication about expectations for their contribution, utilization of their skills, opportunities for growth, access to L&D, and a feeling of belonging. The culture is important here, people need to enjoy their work, they need to feel like they can contribute and have autonomy in their role, and being valued as a person, not just a number, is something that comes up often. A culture like this transforms into a powerful motivator. Employees who have autonomy and creativity in how they solve problems and enact improvements will be motivated intrinsically. Financial rewards ensure the employee feels valued, as well as sharing in the results of productivity gains, and can serve as extrinsic motivation.[1] This combined approach not only enhances talent retention but also purpose and direction in the professional journey of each individual.

Thinking back to our role-mapping exercise, here's another idea you could use that would encourage engagement with your vision and create loyalty and a desire to remain with the business. Some organizations involve employees when deciding what new and existing roles are required in a redesign, essentially letting each employee write their own job description and title.[2] This would require collaboration and an element of democracy to ensure everyone is in agreement, but having been in this position myself before, I can advocate for nothing more motivating than being able to do a job full of the things I love and am good at. This strategy can make our talent feel valued and invested in proving their worth and contributing to achieving the strategy.

There are many other strategies you can include for talent retention, work with the experts in your HR team to align the strategy with progressive, future of work trends that complement your organizational goals.

Here are some additional ideas to enhance our talent retention strategy:

- Automate the boring tasks that no one wants to do. If you can't automate, rotate.
- Regularly benchmark salaries to ensure competitiveness.
- Communicate your purpose and vision, so employees find meaning and value in what they do.
- Design long service awards that hold significant value for employees.
- Ensure any physical workplace has a purpose that provides values, function, and meaning, so employees feel the benefit of being on-site rather than remote.
- Think back to our workplace of the future in Chapter 1; integrate emerging technology into your physical workplace to create a modern, progressive environment.

- Embed practices that regularly praise and celebrate colleagues' achievements, both within and outside the professional realm.
- Explore profit-sharing mechanisms or stock allocation to directly involve employees in the success of the organization.
- Ensure that organizational culture and values are visibly demonstrated by leadership in their behaviors, actions, and decisions.
- Encourage work–life balance and provide paid time off that is at a competitive level.
- Provide growth and learning opportunities.
- Provide competitive benefits, including health care and other perks.
- Implement progressive policies that address various aspects such as adoption leave, parental leave, bereavement support, extended time off for travel, help for menopausal women, or support for domestic violence situations.
- Promote a culture of trust where attendance at personal events like appointments or school plays is expected without the need for explicit prior permission.
- Be a brand or a service that is ethical, does good for the community or the world, that employees can be proud to say they work for.

By integrating these strategies, we aim to not only retain our valuable talent but also redesign our work environment to be one where employees actively contribute to the organizational goals and where the success and well-being of our people are evident.

Working Practices and the Employee Experience

Employee experience is important not only to retain our talent, it's important because in a world that is increasingly moving toward AI and automation, valuing our people is essential for society. Imagine a world, a society, with poverty and crime levels, if all the companies in the world displaced workers in favor of robots. People need to be at the center of our redesign, because yes, passing tasks and processes to robots can give us efficiencies and cost-savings and increased revenue, but robots don't have ambition, creativity, and drive. When making your company successful, it is people that make things happen, and it is people that will make a difference for you.

We need to be aware of the future of work trends, and the research around it, and factor in what we can into our redesign. In sculpting the employee experience, we do need to be forward-thinking and craft a narrative that integrates principles of human-centric automation. This requires a progressive environment, where open communication and trust from the top provides an unwavering commitment to maintaining a positive work environment.

HR and leadership need to have conversations about the employee experience as we work on our transitional action plan. But please, the second someone mentions beanbags and pool tables, kick them right out that door. We want a meaningful employee experience that makes our people want to be here and want to make our vision a reality, which means much more than a fancy break room.

But let's talk about the workplace for a second. Depending on the purpose of your business, we do need to consider this as part of our redesign and how a physical place can contribute to our goals. Information workers, that is those who work from a laptop, can work from anywhere and this is a policy you should consider. There is work from home, work from anywhere, digital nomads where travel and work are encouraged, hybrid work as a mix, and on-site work. I still truly believe in the power of having people together, this builds relationships, sparks creativity, and is effective for collaboration. But does *in-person* need to be a daily activity? If you're making people commute to a workplace to do the exact same thing they can do from their home, then you're not valuing your people or their time. The commute is taking away their opportunity to exercise, enjoy breakfast with their children, and creating barriers for parents or carers who need to do the school run, for example. As well as adding to daily stresses for those people who need to commute home after expending energy at work all day, then still need to shop, clean, cook, care for relatives, and help with homework. If that's their routine every day, how can we expect them to be their most productive, best selves at work? A workplace, and working practices that values people, creates motivated, energized, and loyal workers.

We need to be embracing flexibility that values adaptable work arrangements to effectively balance their professional and personal commitments. This flexibility not only acknowledges the diverse dimensions of modern life but also indicates a sense of autonomy and trust.

In a re-evaluation of the traditional workweek, we should contemplate a shift toward a four-day workweek or reduced working hours to strike a healthier balance between professional and personal life. As we champion work–life balance, our goal is to enhance job satisfaction and overall well-being and the gains we receive from automation should allow us to consider how those productivity gains are shared with our workforce.[3] Just imagine how motivational that could be for employees to help us reach the goals of our redesign, we could achieve huge productivity and efficiency gains by permeating an automation-first strategy into all of our processes, and as an incentive for making this happen, employees end up working less hours for the same pay, with no loss of revenue for the business.

A reduced or compressed workweek isn't just about efficiency; it's a practical approach that enables individuals and the team to achieve more while enjoying extra time outside work. There is evidence of reduced absenteeism, improved mental health, an increase in smarter ways of working leading to being more productive as well as, my favorite, happiness.[4]

The inevitability of AI and automation propels initiatives like a reduced working week, emphasizing the importance of adapting to evolving workplace trends. As automation, robotics, and cognitive technology will do more and more in our working world, futurists and thought leaders are urging a recalibration of what the concept of work means. I'll cover this more in a later chapter, I have lots to say on this.

Remote work also enables you to secure talent from a global talent pool. Distributed teams will help us ensure we have the experts we need to realize our vision, rather than being restricted to recruiting from the local area. This not only taps into a diverse pool of talent with different perspectives and expertise but also reflects our commitment to progressive, competitive working practices.

Redesigning the employee experience should be a collaborative effort, and our people need to be consulted through regular feedback, conversations, or surveys. This ongoing dialogue helps us understand and address the unique needs and aspirations of each individual. This personalized approach creates a rich experience for everyone, enhancing satisfaction, engagement, and personal fulfillment. We need to value every voice, every idea, ensuring that it's heard, considered, and appreciated.

Yes, we're in the era of automation and AI, but I want you to call it the era of human-centric automation. I want you to go beyond pursuing technological advancements and redefine the essence of work and employee engagement. The principles of human-centric automation guide this evolution, emphasizing that technology is a tool to enhance, not replace, human endeavors.

As the organization designs a digital workplace based on human-centric automation, it considers all aspects of how employees interact with technologies, colleagues, and customers. This design not only encourages worker productivity but places humans at the forefront, recognizing them as the organization's biggest asset with deep expertise and creative insights. Engaging employees throughout the design process becomes paramount, ensuring that new automations focus on outcomes for employees as well as customers and the bottom line. This approach harmonizes the principles of human-centric hyperautomation with the overarching narrative of employee well-being, development, and engagement—a testament to the organization's commitment to a future of work defined by fulfillment and success.[5]

Recruitment and Career Planning

As we begin our redesign, organizations can reap enormous benefits from hiring experienced automation developers and leaders externally. We do need individuals with a wealth of deep knowledge, mentorship capabilities, and the ability to establish best practices. Their experience can be instrumental in demonstrating proof of concept and accelerating the implementation of our vision. Whether we hire permanently or borrow this talent as contractors, professionals with this knowledge can be used to implement customized automation solutions, use machine learning and advanced algorithms for transformational projects, and importantly influence the culture essential for a successful organizational redesign.

However, the balance lies in not exclusively relying on external sourcing. The emphasis should be on a mix that also relies on the advantages of internal talent development. We can grow, train, and develop software engineers, automation developers, architects, or analysts internally. This approach not only nurtures internal morale but also shows you value career progression.

Our career management strategies should entail the enablement of cross-functional teams boasting diverse skill sets that can focus on automations or process improvements that add value across multiple business functions. These teams can collaboratively tackle the intricate challenges posed by hyperautomation through experimentation and knowledge sharing. It also helps people experience and empathize with different functional ways of working beyond their original expertise, therefore enhancing their career development options and overall business acumen. Rotating roles is another idea that can create that cross-functional knowledge, again this could be driven by AI systems that monitor and assess achievements and milestones and rotate people, possibly graduates, through various roles and projects based on organizational needs, ensuring continuous growth and engagement.

We can use our talent mapping activity to examine potential within the organization for recruitment into our automation teams, so that we look beyond the traditional source of just IT professionals. Graduates with a strong interest in technology, technology advocates, business process experts, or those in reporting and data intelligence roles—all are potential candidates for the development of an intelligent automation team. Because we don't just want automation to be owned by IT, we want to develop all our people to have digital skills and for automation initiatives to permeate the entire organizational ecosystem. The emphasis is on collaboration with HR and talent specialists to strategically recruit and retain the organization's specialists who can drive our automation vision into the future.

Succession Planning

HR, in collaboration with L&D, play a strategic role in identifying high-potential individuals within the organization and preparing them for the critical roles we have identified. Once we have appointed and mapped people into roles, we also need to consider who might follow them, who needs to be developed and prepped for the eventuality that vacancies become available. Through preparation, we can be responsive to these changes as well as having the added bonus of developing our people with advanced skills.

The concept of succession planning extends beyond individual aspirations; it becomes a strategic recruitment endeavor ensuring that the organization develops a pool of resources capable of filling key positions throughout the maturity journey. The progression from a data administrator to a vacancy as a process analyst or developer, for example, exemplifies how succession planning aligns with recruitment strategy. It not only enriches the talent pool but also contributes significantly to employee experience, reduces recruitment costs, and increases staff retention.

Succession planning should go beyond traditional leadership roles to include positions critical for both automation and our digital transformation projects, such as automation developers, process analysts, data analysts, and change management Specialists. By proactively identifying and developing talent that can succeed into these roles in any eventuality, organizations can ensure a smooth transition of skills and leadership to deliver a long-term realization of our strategy.

Skills Development

As automation takes over routine and repetitive tasks, the focus shifts toward higher-value work that requires digital skills, critical thinking, creativity, and problem-solving abilities. L&D have a lot of work to do here via effective coaching programs, L&D offerings, technical training, and more, to develop the skills we need for the future.

To ensure the workforce remains relevant and adaptable in the age of AI, organizations must prioritize reskilling and upskilling initiatives. Reskilling involves equipping employees with entirely new skill sets to transition to new roles, while upskilling focuses on enhancing existing skills to align with technological advancements. These initiatives enable employees to stay ahead of the curve and contribute meaningfully to business objectives.

Successful reskilling and upskilling programs require a comprehensive and structured approach. L&D should design customized learning paths that cater to individual aspirations, address the results of our skills gap analysis, and align to organizational needs. These paths should include a blend of online and classroom courses, mentoring, practical experience, and certifications. By tailoring education to individual interests as well as role requirements, we can empower employees to acquire the necessary competencies for our AI-powered workplace.

Let's take a look at some L&D programs we may want to consider:

- **Coaching programs**
  - Leaders and managers need to become coaches, guiding their teams through the complexities of automation and instilling a sense of purpose and direction. A coaching program for leaders and managers is crucial to nurturing excellence and cultivating qualities that empower them to lead teams that operate with autonomy, resilience, and innovation.
- **Leadership development**
  - Leadership development programs need to raise the bar in developing leadership qualities of empathy, emotional intelligence, change management, a growth mindset, and collaborative decision-making skills. We need to develop our leaders in such a way that they can inspire and be seen as thought leaders and changemakers in their fields. More on this in the next chapter.
- **Management development**

o   Our people managers, should we decide we need them,
will need to prove their worth by embarking on a development program aimed at driving change, being instigators
and champions of continuous improvement, motivating
high-performance teams, taking ownership of project plans
identified by our strategy, and learning new analytics skills to
take on the changed role of managing both digital co-workers and human co-workers within the same function.

- **People development**
  o   For employees, the need emerges to enhance human
  ingenuity traits that the robots don't have, so as well as
  technical skills we want to deploy initiatives in L&D that
  challenge individuals to engage in critical thinking, problem-
  solving, creativity, process re-engineering, and generally
  approach tasks with innovative design thinking.

- **Learning communities**
  o   Knowledge thrives in collaborative environments, so creating
  learning communities or super user networks where
  employees can share insights, challenges, and solutions can
  work really well. Peer-to-peer mentorship enables experienced individuals to guide and empower their colleagues
  as well as offering encouragement and accountability as the
  group learns new skills together in cohorts. This collaborative wisdom extends beyond the training sessions, creating
  a network where knowledge flows organically, enthused by
  each other's experiences and successes.

- **Digital adoption platforms (DAP)**
  o   Swift technology adoption plays a pivotal role in shaping the
  employee experience and equipping competent employees.
  With so many legacy and new software tools, a DAP is a
  strategy we'd highly recommend you pursue rather than just
  relying on lengthy training courses to learn how to use any
  software. DAPs provide user-friendly tools such as guides,
  knowledge bases, wizards, and walkthroughs embedded
  directly into the software user interface of all applications

to teach employees complex systems at the point of use. This helps with onboarding new colleagues as well as investing in the skills of existing employees to ensure proficiency in utilizing the latest technologies. We don't just provide resources; we provide an environment where technology enhances, not hinders, the employee experience.

- **Agile principles**
  - o Now, let's explore how our very busy L&D teams can guide us in adopting agile work practices. Agile practices involve a flexible approach, focusing on continuous improvement and adaptability to meet evolving business needs. By embracing iterative development processes, we create ways of working that amplify innovation and respond swiftly to changes. L&D led programs should focus on understanding the principles of the agile manifesto, and the teams themselves should be deciding on any frameworks such as dev ops, scrum methodology, or kanban, for example. Scrum may not work with remote, globally distributed teams, and kanban might be more suited to ongoing work projects than deadline-driven product development. There are plenty of delivery models to choose from, what's important first is that people are on-board with the ideology of being agile. Through targeted training, L&D empower teams to operate with agile principles and drive iterative, experimental, and innovative work.[6]

- **Continuous learning culture**
  - o Continuous L&D, not just occasional training offerings, should be a core value within the organizational culture. Regular opportunities for upskilling and reskilling should be provided to ensure employee proficiency aligns with the skills we need to realize our vision. But training isn't there just to reach our goal for the role requirements, we want to ensure that the will and opportunity to learn is a constant, to remain updated as technology evolves and industry needs change, and to ensure our colleagues continue to experi-

ence professional growth. You could consider user-generated content, or unlimited training budgets or enable team members to decide exactly how they spend an allocated training budget; they may prefer books over courses or want to pursue formal certification. Trust your people to know what they need to progress.

- **Organizational change management**
  - Change management should be an integral part of your training and development programs. It's especially important for leaders and change agents, but opening this education out to all can only reap benefits. These initiatives prepare employees for the continuous evolution of their roles in the automation-first environment. Change management training can play a crucial role in maintaining a positive attitude toward change, mitigating change resistance, understanding the psychology and science of change response, and ensuring employees perceive automation as an avenue for growth rather than a threat to job security.

- **Technical training**
  - I'd estimate this part to be a large part of your L&D program as we need to empower our team with the technical expertise essential for the automation era. This begins with tailoring individual, self-paced learning paths to sync with each employee's career aspirations and the role and organizational requirements.
  - The learning approach should combine a blend of state-of-the-art online and classroom courses, immersive hands-on practical sessions, mentorship programs, industry-recognized certifications, vendor-provided training, assignments, group projects, education on ways of working such as design standards, and a safe environment for practice and experimentation. This mix ensures an achievable and well-structured learning path that should start from foundational automation skills moving to advanced proficiency in AI, data science, and machine learning.

- **Automation skills:**
  - Skills needed: Basic understanding of robotic process automation concepts, workflow automation, process mining, and familiarity with automation software.
- **AI:**
  - Skills needed: Knowledge of large language models, neural networks, natural language processing, prompt engineering, use cases, and understanding AI algorithms.
- **Data science:**
  - Skills needed: Data science fundamentals, statistical analysis, advanced analytics, data visualization, predictive modeling, business intelligence, and proficiency in data analytics and visualization software.
- **Machine learning:**
  - Skills needed: In-depth understanding of machine learning and neurolearning algorithms, model evaluation, training a machine learning model with data sets, and optimization techniques.
- **Other technologies:**
  - Skills needed: Other required software for fulfilling the business purpose—for example, ERP systems, customer relationship management, animation software, manufacturing human–machine interfaces, and many more. Each employee needs to be competent in the specific technology needed to excel in their roles. Provide support with the DAP within each application so users can receive tutorials and guidance at the point of use.

Financial Incentives

Yes, we want people who are passionate about learning and getting us to our automation-first utopia. But do not dismiss the power of financial incentives that can serve as catalysts for motivation and achievement. We need to recognize that investing in our employees' learning journeys is an investment in our collective success. By providing monetary rewards tied to skill acquisition and the successful application of new knowledge, we create a culture where continuous learning is not just encouraged but rewarded. Allow employees to earn bonuses or rewards for completing relevant certifications, attending training programs, or successfully showing the value of applying the new skills in their roles. This will accelerate the narrowing of our skills gap and we need to remember that to become a progressive company, we need to embrace progressive learning initiatives. This involves going beyond conventional approaches by incentivizing employees to undertake learning opportunities aligned with their career aspirations and the organization's goals.

AI-Powered Learning and Development

Achieving our vision means embedding AI and automation within every business function, including L&D, and so we should embrace the power of AI and machine learning to personalize learning paths. By leveraging AI algorithms to analyze each employee's strengths, preferences, and growth trajectories, we can guide the creation of tailored learning paths and course suggestions, ensuring that employees experience education that is uniquely suited to their aspirations and the evolving demands of an automation-first environment.

We can introduce AI-powered learning assistants using machine learning algorithms to understand individual learning styles or utilize our own private large language models to offer expertise and answers about our company and products. Serving as virtual tutors, they can provide real-time feedback, competency assessments, suggest relevant learning resources, and provide contextual support based on the learner's progress. This personalized assistance transforms the learning experience, making it adaptive, interactive, and closely aligned with each employee's pace and needs.

We can automate many tasks within the L&D function such as reporting, course enrolments, onboarding, assignments, scheduling, sentiment analysis, and many more use cases. Within every business area, what can be automated, should be automated.

In summary, by prioritizing reskilling and upskilling initiatives, enthusing a culture of continuous learning, and deploying DAPs, organizations can empower their workplace to thrive in the era of intelligent automation. The journey toward human–AI synergy is not without its challenges, but with the right strategies and approaches, L&D teams can help drive success for our transformation.

Reward, Remuneration, and Recognition

The traditional approaches in this area also need to undergo a progressive transformation[7]. Let's explore some ways in which we can redesign our reward programs to motivate and engage employees in our new world.

- Salaries
    - Salaries not only need to be competitive, they also need to reflect the value that employees provide, from their own perspective. Consider transparent salary ranges or even adopting a democratic approach to deciding bonuses and salaries, involving employees in the decision-making process.
    - If you have the data to calculate your gender pay gap, you already know who is affected and how much is needed to close it. Instead of celebrating incremental progress, take action and fix it.
- Profit sharing and employee ownership
    - Explore ways to directly involve employees in the success of the company. This includes profit-sharing mechanisms, co-operative ownership or stock allocation, where employees have a stake in the organization's performance.
- Automation impact bonuses:
    - Introduce bonuses for employees whose contributions to AI and automation initiatives lead to substantial efficiency gains, cost savings, or significant improvements in business processes. This directly links financial rewards to the tangible impact of automation efforts.
    - Offer incentives to submit ideas to the intelligent automation pipeline, with a further award given if the idea and benefit come to fruition.

- Innovation grants:
  - o Establish a fund that employees can access to support large innovative projects or ideas related to the use of cognitive technologies. This financial reward can empower employees to pursue creative solutions that contribute to the organization's goals and potentially, to being seen as a changemaker in your industry.
- Retention bonuses:
  - o Retain skilled employees by offering retention bonuses based on years' service or completing projects. This is particularly relevant for individuals with specialized knowledge, ensuring that the organization retains this expertise.
- Milestone-based rewards:
  - o Introduce financial rewards tied to the achievement of specific milestones in projects. Whether it's completing a crucial phase, surpassing performance targets, or successfully integrating new technologies, employees receive bonuses as they contribute to the organization's digital transformation journey.
- Benefit packages:
  - o Offer competitive benefit packages typical to your industry but also assess how you can go further in attracting and retaining top talent.
  - o Some organizations are now offering housing subsidies, student loan support, time off for birthdays and weddings, caregiver benefits[8], travel allowances, sabbaticals, free holiday locations[9], and financial well-being programs, among others.
- Recognition programs:
  - o Publicly acknowledge and celebrate milestones, innovations, and contributions to the automation-first journey.
  - o Similarly, encourage the continuous learning culture by celebrating employees who complete training and certification programs.
  - o Host annual award programs nominated by their peers for internal recognition.

o   Provide budget and time for entering external awards relevant to your industry.

o   Create and encourage communication channels dedicated to praising and thanking colleagues.

Organizations must embrace continuous improvement and adaptation in their reward programs. This includes exploring new and impactful benefits, and staying attuned to the changing needs and expectations of employees. By constantly refining and adapting reward programs, organizations can create a dynamic and engaging work environment that attracts and retains top talent.

Diversity, Ethics, and Inclusion

To unlock our organization's full potential, we must value diversity, ethics, and inclusion. HR and L&D can utilize policies, as well as AI algorithms, to detect and eliminate biases in talent acquisition, reskilling, and career progression, ensuring equal opportunities for all.

Diversity isn't just a checkbox; it drives innovation using different perspectives and experiences.

Ethical considerations extend far beyond our people policies, within our technological efforts ethical principles must be integrated into policies and procedures, empowering employees to make transparent and ethical decisions regarding AI's impact on privacy, security, and data integrity.

Inclusivity also needs to be at the forefront of leadership strategy, remembering that our culture and values need to be visible from the top down. The organizational hierarchy should be a reflection of our diversity and represent a myriad of voices and perspectives. Investing in diverse leadership development programs shows a commitment to nurturing qualities like empathy, diversity appreciation, social mobility, and collaborative decision making. These programs don't just create leaders; they cultivate inclusive leaders who are adept at steering organizations through the complexities of an automated future.

Recommended Roles Required

The foundations of an automation-first organization lie in its team structure. The crafting of roles within the organization should be executed with care and precision, with an eye on the future, to ensure a dedicated focus on automation implementation, digital transformation, and continuous improvement.

At the inception of a hyperautomation transformation, you might not need all of these roles, your teams might have the capacity to look after multiple responsibilities. For example, your developers may do process analysis, documentation, building, and then test the solution all themselves. This versatility is beneficial, especially when resources can cover multiple tasks during the initial phases. However, as capability grows, a more specialized and dedicated resource for each skill becomes a strategic imperative.

Table 9.2 lists typical roles you may want to consider in your role mapping exercise and are suited to organizations pursuing digital transformation and an AI-first redesign.

Navigating the Future of Work

As organizations navigate the future of work, a strategy for talent and roles in the AI-powered workplace stands as a critical determinant of success. The collaboration between HR, L&D, and talent management becomes the stimulus for engaging and developing our people and transforming not only the technical landscape but the very culture of the organization.

Table 9.2 Recommended roles

Title	Description
AI ethics specialist	The AI ethics specialist ensures that artificial intelligence (AI) integration aligns with ethical standards. Responsibilities include assessing ethical impacts, identifying AI model biases, and implementing measures to address ethical concerns. The AI ethics specialist promotes responsible and ethical automation practices, ensuring alignment with moral and societal values.
Automation architect	Overseeing essential aspects of automation implementation. Responsibilities include product setup, installation, updates, and ensuring a functioning and secure automation environment. The automation architect manages system backups and the technical infrastructure and databases necessary for optimal performance.
Automation administrator	The automation administrator oversees the day-to-day performance of automated solutions managing their uptime, service-level agreements, scheduling, reporting, pursues AI monitoring, and serves as a central point for coordinating automation activities and optimizing the efficiency of your digital co-workers.
Automation developer	The developers are the key players in our automation initiatives, tasked with building the automated solution and integrating AI or ML as required. This role requires technical skills as well as a grasp of the overall business context. Collaborating with various stakeholders, including process analysts and business process owners, the developer ensures the automated solution accurately reflects the requirements as well as providing the maximum benefits and improvements that automation can offer.
Automation testers	Testers undertake the responsibility of thoroughly testing the automated processes to ensure they meet the defined criteria, are free from defects, and have been tested on real-world scenarios. This role involves creating and implementing test scripts, identifying and documenting issues, and collaborating with developers to resolve defects, ensuring that the automated solution functions seamlessly.
Business analyst	A business analyst is responsible for evaluating and optimizing an organization's documentation, processes, and systems. They analyze data, communicate with stakeholders, and provide valuable insights to support informed decision making. Business

(Continued)

Table 9.2 (*Continued*)

Title	Description
	analysts play a key role in enhancing overall efficiency and effectiveness within an organization by identifying areas for improvement, providing detailed documentation, and proposing solutions to drive positive change.
Business process owner	The business process owner will own and optimize specific business processes, ensuring they align with key deliverables. Collaborating with stakeholders, responsibilities include managing entire business processes, ensuring compliance, identifying improvements, and driving overall efficiency in the move to automated processes.
Change management specialists	Change management specialists guide the organization through cultural and systemic shifts. This role includes developing strategies to handle resistance, communicating changes effectively, and ensuring a seamless transition for employees affected by automation or other projects.
Chief AI officer	A chief AI officer (CAIO) leads the strategic integration of artificial intelligence within an organization, ensuring that AI-driven solutions align with business objectives and enhance decision making, efficiency, and innovation. A CAIO is essential to spearhead the adoption of AI technologies, manage ethical considerations, and position the organization at the forefront of digital evolution.
Continuous improvement lead	As the driving force behind efficiency, the continuous improvement lead analyses performance metrics, identifies improvement areas, and implements enhancements to optimize projects, teams, ways of working, and automated processes. They are crucial enablers for a culture of innovation and could be the perfect role to oversee digital twin simulations and predictive analytics to ensure we make the most impactful improvement steps.
Cybersecurity analyst	The cybersecurity analyst focuses on fortifying IT solutions, including our automations, against potential threats, vulnerabilities, and cyberattacks. This role involves assessing the security position, implementing encryption measures, and staying

(*Continued*)

Table 9.2 (Continued)

Title	Description
	abreast of the latest cybersecurity trends and threats. Machine learning and AI predictive analysis can help with threat detection and response testing here.
Data analyst/scientist	The data analyst plays a vital role in extracting valuable insights from data generated by all our IT systems with perhaps a dedicated role just to focus on data from our automated processes. This should involve utilizing machine learning and AI systems for analyzing patterns and trends for data-driven decision making and strategies that leverage automation for maximum impact.
Data governance lead	The data governance leads oversee data quality, integrity, and compliance. This role ensures that data used in the business adheres to quality standards, regulatory requirements, and organizational policies.
Data visualization specialist	The data Visualization specialist transforms complex data into visual representations for easy interpretation. This role is crucial for communicating insights and key performance indicators in automation. Collaborating with analysts and decision makers, the specialist creates visually compelling dashboards, facilitating better understanding and informed decision making.
Delivery or program lead	The delivery lead is a key player in establishing the delivery capability within the organization. Working closely with the head of automation and the IT team, the delivery lead ensures smooth program management covering methodologies, roles, responsibilities, governance, training programs, certification programs, and technical infrastructure.
Head of automation	The head of automation is the strategic leader responsible for managing the IA program or the center of excellence (CoE) across the business. With a focus on aligning automated processes with operational requirements, the head of automation ensures the optimal business benefit and evangelizes about the possibilities. Leadership responsibilities encompass strategic ownership of the entire delivery model and scaling automation throughout the business.

(Continued)

Table 9.2 (Continued)

Title	Description
HR lead	HR owns the policy and procedural requirements for all our people's needs. They need to drive the strategy for our organizational transformation and employee experience goals. The future of this role should encompass predictive analytics to foresee and mitigate potential employee burnout, disengagement, skill shortages, or turnover.
Information officer	The information officer role, or data privacy officer, oversees both the organization's information strategy and the safeguarding of sensitive data. Responsible for managing data governance, information security, and compliance with data protection regulations and audits, this role ensures the responsible use of information in the business and in the context of automation.
Innovation lead	The innovation lead focuses on driving technological advancements, exploring emerging technologies, and industry trends and ways of working. This role ensures that the organization stays at the forefront of innovation, leveraging new technologies to enhance automation or organizational capabilities and performance.
Internal communications	Working closely with change management specialists, this role will communicate automation-related or other changes to employees. Nurturing a transparent and supportive communication strategy can benefit from natural language processing (NLP) to capture sentiment analysis and real-time engagement levels.
IT lead	The head of IT or IT lead role extends beyond automation, encompassing all facets of information technology. They own the strategic vision for IT, ensuring seamless integration with our business objectives, overseeing the IT infrastructure, cloud strategies, cybersecurity, and the implementation of cutting-edge technologies that drive efficiency and innovation ensuring our IT ecosystem aligns with the dynamic needs of the business.
Knowledge management specialist	The knowledge management specialist focuses on capturing, organizing, and disseminating institutional knowledge. This role ensures that valuable insights and learnings are documented and shared to support continuous improvement. This role can

(Continued)

Table 9.2 (Continued)

Title	Description
	work with digital adoption platforms and AI-driven analytics to predict the information people will need and when they will need it.
Learning and development (L&D) lead	The L&D lead will focus on empowering skill development, performance, and growth in our people. They will design and implement initiatives that enhance the skills and knowledge of our workforce, embrace innovation including personalized AI learning initiatives, and contribute to the continuous technical prowess and professional development of our workforce.
Machine learning engineer	The machine learning engineer develops algorithms for predictive analysis and self-learning within automated processes. Collaborating with developers, analysts, and ethics specialists, this role ensures alignment and adds a predictive dimension to automation, data, and enabling the organization to anticipate future challenges and change impact.
Project management office (PMO) specialist	During a large business change program, a PMO function is recommended to manage the budget, resource, reporting, and governance needs of multiple projects. This serves to ensure projects remain aligned to business objectives and prioritized accordingly.
Process analyst	The process analyst is responsible for identifying and assessing AI use cases and automation opportunities and owns all the documentation requirements, collaborating with the business and the developers. They are pivotal in driving process re-engineering to ensure the solution delivers the required benefits realization. They should be utilizing and advocating for best practice using advanced technology like digital twin simulations, AI-driven analytics, process mining, and machine learning, in order to suggest the most efficient ways for processes to be executed.
Software testers	When implementing or developing other nonautomation new technologies, software testers play a crucial role in ensuring the quality of the product. They are responsible for conducting thorough tests to validate that the implemented software meets

(Continued)

Table 9.2 (Continued)

Title	Description
	defined criteria and is free from defects. The goal is to ensure that the software functions consistently perform and align with business requirements. This role should be utilizing automated testing where possible.
Solution architect	The solution architect is responsible for designing and overseeing the implementation of high-level structures for all IT systems. Their role involves understanding requirements and translating them into an architecture that guides the roadmap and vision. This includes providing technical guidance, evaluating new technologies, ensuring quality standards, and defining system components, modules, interfaces, and data for a solution that aligns with business goals, scalability, security, and performance requirements.
Talent management specialists	Talent management specialists are responsible for identifying and acquiring individuals with unique skills that contribute to our vision. AI can be used to forecast the future skill needs of the organization for future workforce planning. They also nurture the potential of and endeavor to retain our existing talent to ensure that our teams are equipped to meet organizational goals.
User experience (UX) designer	The UX designer focuses on improving the interaction between humans and automated systems, or between users and software products. This role entails designing user-friendly interfaces, conducting feedback sessions, and optimizing the user journey to ensure a seamless and user-friendly experience, promoting adoption and satisfaction.
	Note: Other roles may be required to support the specifics of your business and industry, such as customer experience specialists, supply change leads, safety, regulatory, or sustainability roles among many others.

CHAPTER 10

Shifting Mindsets for Successful Adoption

Intelligent automation holds immense promise for transforming the way businesses operate, but successful implementation requires effective change management. To achieve the full potential of cognitive computing, organizations must ensure that their employees are engaged in the redesign, equipped to adapt to the transition, and have a deep understanding of the changes that lie ahead. In this chapter, we will explore the critical role of change management in intelligent automation projects and outline key strategies for driving successful adoption.

Stakeholder Identification

Who should be consulted in our change management activities? First and foremost, involving employees from the beginning is critical to shifting mindsets. Employees are the ones who will be most affected by the changes, so it is crucial to get their input and feedback early on. By involving employees, you can identify potential issues and address them before they become significant problems but in addition, by involving them you make them feel valued to the organization and to the outcomes of the project. Representatives from our employees are the first people we ask to help us with the below activities.

We also need to identify other stakeholders that we may want to invite to contribute to the sections most relevant to them. Plot a list of leaders who have power or influence to make decisions and changes within the business, also include leaders whose business areas are most impacted, as well as any subject matter experts in the technology capabilities. These lists of stakeholders should be consulted or informed throughout our change plan, as well as be recipients of our communication plan.

Change Impact Analysis

Conducting a change impact analysis is essential to help you understand the potential impacts of the change on your organization. We should focus on people primarily but also include changes to processes, policies, ways of working, and systems. We can feed into this any risk management activities, the results of our role mapping exercise, the assessment gap analysis we completed, and anything else that either our employees or stakeholders deem relevant.

The purpose is to identify what the change impact is (a change being a difference to the current status quo), how probable the change impact is likely to happen, whether the level of impact is high, medium, or low, and finally what interventions we can take to lessen or mitigate the impact.

Note: We may not always be able to mitigate the impact, but when we can't, we use honesty and transparency clearly articulating business reasons, and we consider what support can be offered (Table 10.1).

1. **Define change scope:**
   - Articulate the scope of the change, specifying the areas and business functions that will be impacted by the shift to an automation-first approach.
   - Note: We do want to scale automation across the business, but at this stage, if it is a phased approach, specify the business areas for the first phases.
2. **Identify business process impacts:**
   - List and identify the key business processes or functions that are likely to undergo changes due to the automation initiative.
   - Identify the number of processes likely to be converted to automation or AI.
   - Indicate the criticality of the processes.
3. **Identify technology impacts:**

Table 10.1 Change impact analysis

Who		What						Type of impact	How	Comments
Department impacted	Roles impacted	What is the impact	As-is	To-be	Probability (H/M/L)	Impact level L/M/H	Score	People/process / technology, and so on	What intervention is needed to support the change	
		Description								

- List and identify the legacy systems no longer required, or that require significant development or upgrades.
- Identify any impact on data, interfaces, infrastructure, or integrations.

4. **Identify people and role impacts:**
   - Identify people who will be affected by the change. This includes everyone from front-line employees to managers and executives.
   - Specify the roles that will undergo changes, requiring reskilling, upskilling, or potentially becoming redundant with the introduction of automation. Also, include any changes to contracts, or hours.
   - Identify how any changes in organizational structure are going to have an effect. Identify changes in reporting lines, hierarchies, locations, or departmental functions.

5. **Assess future state impact:**
   - Include an impact if the culture and values of the organization don't align with the *to-be* state.
   - Discuss the potential impact of the future state on each area for people, process, and technologies, considering the introduction of automation technologies.
   - Ensure all stakeholders are aware and informed on what the change will realistically mean to the organization, the scale of it, and the effort to address any pain points or obstacles.

6. **Degree of impact:**
   - Clearly define what constitutes a high, medium, or low impact ensuring agreement among stakeholders on the criteria, considering factors like the number of affected individuals, the gap from *as-is* to the *to-be*, the criticality of the function/process or the significance of the change on business objectives.
   - Quantify the degree of impact for each impact identified.

7. **Probability of impact:**

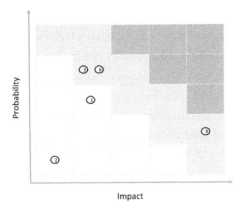

Figure 10.1 Change impact analysis

- Clearly define what constitutes a high, medium, or low probability, ensuring agreement among stakeholders on the criteria.
- Assess and quantify the likelihood that the impact will be experienced as described.

8. **Priority of impact analysis:**
   - Score both the impact and probability columns ($H = 9$, $M = 3$, $L = 1$).
   - Plot the impact scores on a chart for visibility (see Figure 10.1).
   - Multiply Impact × Probability.
   - Ensure the table is sorted in order of priority being the highest total.
   - Agree and refine the priority order, it may be that one business function has the most impacts identified; although classified as medium, it will indicate to us that this particular area will need close support.

9. **Intervention strategies:**
   - Propose interventions needed to support each identified change impact, outlining specific actions required for successful adaptation to the new automation-first environment.

- Consider how you can mitigate the impacts to reduce the likelihood of experiencing operational disruption or risks to the project timeline or outcomes.
- Provide space for additional comments or qualitative insights that can enhance the understanding of the impact and associated considerations.

10. **Review and validation:**
- Engage key stakeholders in the review process, validating the identified impacts, ratings, and proposed interventions. Incorporate feedback for accuracy.

11. **Continuous refinement:**
- Acknowledge that the change impact analysis is iterative. Continuously refine and update the analysis as the automation-first initiative progresses.

The proposed interventions, which might be comms, policy changes, training, testing, or business readiness preparation, for example, then need to be included in an action plan. I would recommend including in the same action plan you are using for project planning. The change management lead may be facilitating these actions, but it will be leadership and managers, and potentially change agents, who will own the actions and we need to ensure these results are given the importance and visibility they deserve.

Change Management Assessment Tools

Heatmapping: Employ a change heatmapping approach to visually represent the number of and level of impact per business function, including the combined impact of any other ongoing changes and projects. This entails assessing the amount of change in different business areas, bringing to light who may have the most high-impact changes and therefore need more support, or any business function undergoing too much change at once or pinpointing potential areas of resistance. This gauges the overall organizational readiness for a major transformation. This method allows organizations to proactively identify and address change fatigue and strategically sequence initiatives for optimal outcomes.

Persona profiling: Think of this as creating fictional characters to represent employees in different parts of your workplace. When implementing changes, consider how they will affect different people. This exercise helps anticipate how changes might impact individuals, considering their reactions and sentiments. It provides insights to address the unique needs of different groups and ensures a more empathetic, tailored approach to support during the transformation.

Employee surveys: Implementing employee surveys is a vital tool to gauge the pulse of the organization during periods of change. These surveys, aligned with methodologies like the Prosci® ADKAR model, allow you to systematically assess employees' awareness, desire, knowledge, ability, and reinforcement concerning the change. By collecting feedback and understanding the specific challenges or concerns employees may have, we can tailor the change management strategies more effectively.

Case for change sessions: This session is an excellent opportunity to encourage buy-in, gain key insights, and demonstrate your utopian vision. Invite key stakeholders and representatives from impacted departments to present your case for change. Discuss the current challenges with the workload, processes, or ways of working (the *as-is* process) and articulate the future *to-be* vision. During this session, it's crucial to have the project sponsor or senior leader be a host and answer any questions. Include an activity where participants split into groups or breakout rooms to produce an "elevator pitch" for the benefits of cognitive computing and how it will help achieve company goals, this exercise can help gain support for the overall aims of the project. You should next invite contributions from participants to capture the detail of how people, processes, and technology, will be impacted by the change—feed this into your change impact analysis. Educate attendees on your change management strategy and key fundamental principles of change and change resistance. Finally, solicit suggestions on what the communication and training plans should consist of; by involving users in the learning design and preferences we create engaged employees who are subconsciously invested in seeing the initiatives they suggested be a success.[1]

Change Agents and Super Users

Change agents are an effective resource to act as evangelists for our cause, be a conduit for communications, and own the change actions for their relevant business area. Super users play the combined role of change agents as well as expert coaches in system usage.

Inspirational leadership must give a top-down mandate, but we also need a grassroots initiative to drive the change from the bottom up, simply because the people doing the work have the best knowledge of what's needed to enact change.

1. Recruit:

- Following the initial stages of your communications plan, the organization should now be aware of your vision. At this stage, you can advertise for volunteers to be change agents or super users, giving an attractive description of what it will entail and the benefits for both them and the organization.
- Look for the people who are already excited about the possibilities that AI and automation will bring, and approach them directly.
- Identify those people who are passionate about technology and have digital skills and a desire to learn and develop themselves.
- Speak to HR and your department heads about who's considered "talent" in the different areas of the business.
- Aim for good coverage among seniority levels, departments, and experience.

2. Educate:

- Educate them on what cognitive technologies involve: ensure they can speak confidently about digital co-workers, the software, what can be automated, and what benefits AI will bring.
- Upskill them on change management principles such as the technology adoption curve, change curve, and mitigating change resistance.
- Have them shadow or spend time with your automation Center Of Excellence (CoE) team to understand more about how automations will be designed and built.
- Provide them with a playbook on activities and interventions they can host to improve change acceptance, and common responses to questions or concerns.

3. Deploy:

- Give them tasks, such as conducting the **case-for-change** sessions with their teams, to evangelize about the possibilities with automation and reinforce the compelling vision and goals for the project.
- Consider using change management tools such as the Prosci ADKAR method to survey all their colleagues on their *awareness, desire,* and *knowledge* about automation.
- Assign actions from our impact action plan as well as actions to work on improving survey scores and reducing resistance in their relevant areas.
- Use them as a conduit for your communications: have them pass on key messages and provide a feedback loop, so you can factor in current feelings and responses into your future comms and change initiatives.
- Have them join process discovery workshops to discuss potential projects and identify processes that will be ideal candidates for automation.
- Involve them in the testing and piloting of your solutions.
- Give them the responsibility of training others in their departments if ways of working are changed.

- Use their influencing skills to be a voice of best practices around the business to encourage adoption in others.
- Utilize them to create engaging campaigns, perhaps naming the digital co-worker in their teams, or having a leaderboard of activities or savings to date, to compete between other agents or departments.
- Empower them to come up with their ideas to influence successful change.

4. Develop:

- Give them the tools and training to consider how current processes can be re-engineered: either to be better candidates for automation or to ensure people and digital co-workers are collaborating as co-workers in a harmonized manner.
- Name them in your succession plans for your CoE roles—if they have the desire to be a process analyst or developer in the future, help with the upskilling and career development to make this a possibility in the future.
- Give them the responsibility for benefits realization, data visualization, or reporting for their areas.
- Have your sponsor or other senior leaders publicly recognize their efforts with thanks, rewards, credibility boosts, or incentivization.
- Provide them with career opportunities to boost their profile. For example, to present to the board on automation progress or to host open days or roadshows for other colleagues to learn more about AI and automation.
- Encourage them to participate in networking opportunities with senior leaders, CoE teams, and others externally in the intelligent automation space to share knowledge, best practices, and instigate new ideas for automation growth to scale and transform your business.[2]

Change Management Education

Change education involves educating leadership, key stakeholders, change agents, people managers, and your intelligent automation delivery team, on the core principles of change management. By equipping these individuals with the tools and knowledge they need to act as change drivers, you can influence the successful implementation and adoption of intelligent automation.

Here are some topics you can include in your educational sessions:

- An introduction to the fundamental principles of change management and its necessity in the context of achieving our vision.
- Discuss case studies of organizational change, drawing examples from both within and outside the organization. Highlight instances like Betamax, Kodak, BlackBerry, Blockbusters, and Myspace, showcasing the consequences of failing to adapt to digital transformation.
- Conduct brainstorming sessions on why our organizational change initiative might fail, often referred to rather morosely as premortem analysis, as this will help you identify factors to mitigate.
- Deepen the understanding of how the brain processes change. "A different part of the brain handles all routine tasks and uses little energy, from the part of the brain that processes our response to change and uses a lot of energy. Our brain is designed to conserve energy, which is why we are hardwired to avoid change."[3] Emphasize that change resistance is a natural human response, and forcing change can induce anxiety.
- Recognize that humans are generally more averse to losses than they are motivated by potential gains. When discussing automation with team members, attendees should emphasize the gains and benefits but also address perceived losses.
- Cultivate emotional intelligence by empathizing with the emotional responses of individuals going through the change process. Emotions such as fear, uncertainty, and resistance are

natural. Responding with empathy and support helps build trust and a positive atmosphere.

Providing change management education to key players is crucial for the successful implementation and adoption of intelligent automation. By introducing key principles, discussing case studies, and understanding the psychology of change, you can equip your team with the knowledge and tools they need to act as change agents, so they can have supportive conversations about the new technology and ways of working.

Mitigating Change Resistance

Change is an inevitable part of life, and it is no different in the world of business. As technology advances, companies must adapt quickly to stay ahead of the competition, and that is why many of us get excited about the transformational value that cognitive computing can bring. However, not everyone in the company may be on board with the changes, and this is where change resistance can make or break your project.

I've seen plenty of examples of new technology coming along over the years that caused resistance, controversy, or worry. I remember the worry of jobs changing when we introduced PCs to replace the typewriters in what was then known as the typing pool, all women of course. I remember having to persuade salesmen, yes all men back then too, to leave their paper diaries and product catalogs at home as I could give them everything they needed at the touch of a button. There was pushback from retail store managers who couldn't see the value of a website for shopping, and resistance when handheld telephones were removed from desks as communication moved online. Today, all of that technology is widely accepted, and in hindsight, the fears seem unwarranted—AI will likely follow a similar path. However, in the moment, change resistance feels very real. So how did we overcome it? By listening to employees, explaining the reasons behind the changes, and providing retraining for the new technology.

Change resistance can manifest in different ways. Some people may seem hesitant, disengaged, or indifferent, their expertise or status may be perceived as being challenged causing defensiveness, while others may express frustration or make negative comments about the implementation. People may also avoid using new software systems, or attending training, or avoid suggesting processes for automation, gatekeeping them to prevent their tasks from changing.

It's important to recognize the signs of change resistance and address them before they become a bigger issue. Here are some potential responses and mitigations to change resistance:

1. Ensure communication plans have relayed the vision, benefits, project plan, and training plan to all employees. Clear and transparent communication can help people understand the reasoning behind the change and the benefits that it can bring.

2. Listen to people and provide opportunities for opinions to be discussed. Make employees feel heard and valued, and take their feedback into account when making decisions. Resistance is not always negative, and people may raise valid concerns that need to be addressed as part of our impact analysis.

3. Address any unfounded fears or concerns and debunk any myths.

4. Request input from employees if they have expert advice or suggestions. This can help by ensuring people feel their contributions are welcome and assist investment and ownership in the project.

5. Provide more information or FAQs. The more information people have, the better they can understand the project and its implications.

6. Host an intelligent automation demonstration and Q&A. Seeing the technology in action can help to alleviate any concerns or fears people may have.

7. Host a race during your demonstration with a key supporter of automation completing a process manually in competition with a digital co-worker and see who does it quicker. It's important

when doing this activity to ask the volunteers to voice what they are now going to do with the time they have saved. It needs to be presented in a positive light.

8. Have senior leaders reinforce key messages. Seeing support from higher-ups can help to increase credibility, trust, and engagement with the project.

9. Use change agents to talk to people, feed this back to you, and strategically convey reassuring messages in response.

10. Be honest about past project pain that did not go well. Communicate the lessons learned or how the project will be done differently this time around.

11. Be transparent about any job changes or training opportunities that will come with the automation. Let employees know how they will be impacted and what support they will receive.

12. Mine employees who are experts on current technology for process information for your opportunities pipeline.

By recognizing change resistance and taking steps to address it, you can increase engagement, shift mindsets, and enhance buy-in for your intelligent automation project, making the implementation process smoother and more successful.

Enablement and Adoption

Digital co-workers will alter how you work and the types of work your employees will be doing. You will need to consider your cultural adoption as well as user adoption of the technology. This will adapt over time as you introduce newer ways of working and different types of technology so this will need to be worked on continuously as adoption is one of the biggest success factors to your program.

The following suggestions can have a positive impact on adoption, work with change management leads and change agents to add new suggestions to your toolkit.

Leadership playbook for automation:

- Develop a leadership playbook for automation, outlining specific actions, messaging, and behaviors expected from leaders at each stage of the change process.

Confidential support forums:

- Collaborate with external coaching or counseling services to provide confidential one-on-one sessions for employees navigating significant changes.

Podcasts or webinars:

- Launch a bi-monthly podcast or webinar series exploring the evolution of work, the impact of digital co-workers, and the future of automation. Engage leaders, employees, and invite guest thought-leaders to share insights and success stories, promoting a deeper understanding of automation's role within the organization.

Business function workshops:

- Conduct monthly interactive sessions targeted at specific business functions, in turn, to propose potential use cases, educate and demystify automation, and do deep-dive sessions or proof of concept demonstrations into specific business processes.
- Remember to consider competitions or incentives for suggesting potential use cases to populate your pipeline.

Leadership townhall:

- Leaders should champion and include any automation narrative in leadership town hall meetings to address queries live, provide updates, and celebrate successes.

Humanizing digital co-workers:

- Encourage people to name the AI workers in their team, give them an image, and utilize storytelling techniques that showcase success stories and the positive impacts of automation on their work.

Manifesto for human-centric values:

- Develop a manifesto that reinforces the organization's commitment to a people-first approach, a collaborative workforce, and that automation is there to enhance the work we do, not replace the workers.

A day in the life of:

- Initiate a monthly *day in the life of automation team* feature. Allow team members to showcase their work, educating others on their roles, the impact of their work, and the benefits brought by AI and automation.

Automation innovation hub:

- Establish an online automation innovation hub equipped with tools and resources.
- Provide access to keystroke recording software to enable people to capture the steps in a process before submitting them as a potential automation opportunity.
- Include educational content into the fundamentals of the tech and the factors that make a process a viable candidate for using cognitive technology.
- Provide a decision flow chart for people to understand what processes should be added to your pipeline.
- Guide employees on how to submit ideas to the automation pipeline, emphasizing any incentives for doing so.
- Provide access to dashboards, updates, and reporting related to reengineered processes.
- Host competitions or *hackathons* to invite solutions to problems or to build an automation to solve a particular challenge.

- Include online forums or discussion boards dedicated to automation discussions.
- Allow people to upvote potential automation ideas to crowd-source your pipeline intelligence.
- Provide access to knowledge articles, courses, and learning opportunities about intelligent automation. Don't put barriers in the way of learning, if someone wants to learn how to automate even though it's not required for their role, give them access to the online resources.
- Encourage employees to experiment with automation ideas or generative AI, nurturing a grassroots approach to innovation.

Automation excellence awards ceremony:

- Introduce an annual automation excellence awards ceremony to recognize and celebrate outstanding contributions.

Employee feedback surveys:

- Conduct quarterly employee surveys focused on automation. Collect insights to tailor communication strategies, address concerns proactively, and ensure continuous improvement.

Pilot programs:

- Implement pilot programs to test automation initiatives on a smaller scale and provide proof of concept.
- Replicate pilot programs in other business functions to assess the feasibility to scale.
- Gather lessons learned to refine strategies and address challenges before scaling fully throughout the organization.

Citizen developer programs:

- Establish programs to empower employees to operate as citizen developers who can autonomously build simple solutions that automate their own work or tasks in their own department. (Remember, the large, complex, or cross-functional automations should only be built by the team of experienced full-time developers.)

- Provide resources and training to enable them to contribute to automation initiatives and thus scale it throughout our organization.

Business Readiness

It's not enough to just introduce new automation practices to your business, you need to know if your business is prepared for them to succeed. By completing a thorough review of the people, process, and technology components crucial to the adoption of adoption, we can enhance confidence and shift mindsets to prime acceptance and success before putting any projects live.

This is an example of a business readiness assessment that you could tailor to your own organization. Include a RAG rating (red = criteria not met, amber = concerns in meeting criteria, green = criteria met) to provide a visual and meet or discuss regularly to enable escalation of any issues (Table 10.2).

Conduct a Go/No-Go Meeting to Evaluate Readiness:

Organize a Go/No-Go meeting specifically focused on evaluating the readiness. During this meeting, assess the team's comprehension of their roles, their ability to handle issues, and their familiarity with escalation procedures. Make the Go decision only when confident in the team's preparedness.

This structured approach to the Go/No-Go business readiness meeting and subsequent operational readiness ensures a methodical and confident transition to the live production phase of automation projects.

The meeting outputs can be categorized into three distinct possibilities:

1. Go: The project receives the green light to proceed with the live production phase.

Table 10.2 Business readiness

Readiness factor PEOPLE	Success criteria	RAG rating	Comments
Leadership alignment and commitment	# confirmed	Red Amber Green	Use this column to indicate if a red rating indicates an automatic no-go decision
CoE roles fully recruited, defined, and in place	Y/N		
CoE fully trained or certified	% complete		
Communication plan executed	# of campaigns completed		
Employee education completed	Handbook/pipeline information distributed		
Change agent coverage	# per business function		
Change management education completed	# of leaders/change agents required		
Change impact critical actions completed	Survey ratings at expected level or # actions completed		
Role and contract changes completed	# of critical roles or Y/N		
Operational team informed of Go-Live and responsibilities	Y/N		(for automation going live)
Hypercare roles and responsibilities defined	Y/N		(for automation going live)
Readiness factor PROCESS	**Success criteria**	**RAG rating**	**Comments**
Automation and AI opportunities in pipeline	# in pipeline	Red Amber Green	
Pipeline assessed for feasibility, simplicity, impact, and priority	Y/N		
Process analysis completed and benefits identified	Y/N		
Processes selected for AI augmentation or automation build	Y/N		

(Continued)

Table 10.2 (Continued)

Readiness factor PROCESS	Success criteria	RAG rating	Comments
Process documentation in place	Y/N		
Selected process assessed for re-engineering	Y/N		
Project plan or cutover plan complete	% complete		
Disaster recovery and contingency planning in place	Y/N		
Responsibilities agreed for human and digital co-workers for process	Y/N		
Process owner and operational team trained	Y/N		
Procedure in place for how human co-workers will process any errors or cases that the digital co-worker cannot	Y/N		
Risk management and mitigation	% with mitigation actions identified/executed		
Readiness factor TECHNOLOGY	Success criteria	RAG rating	Comments
Infrastructure in place	Y/N		
Software access and permissions completed	# CoE with access		
Digital co-worker access and permissions completed	# live and ready digital co-workers		
Selected solution tested with no defects	Y/N or # of acceptable defects remaining		
Application environment ready for automation deployment	Y/N		
IT and vendor support model in place	Y/N		

(Continued)

Table 10.2 (Continued)

Readiness factor TECHNOLOGY	Success criteria	RAG rating	Comments
User acceptance testing complete	Business acceptance Y/N		
Regression testing complete on linked processes or systems	Y/N		
Data and security policies in place	Y/N		
Computer systems validation plan completed	Y/N		

2. No-Go: The project is put on hold due to identified reasons for noncompliance or potential risks. Record the reasons for the No-Go decision.
3. Go with caveats: Specific aspects of the project can proceed, provided that identified caveats are reconciled within a set period.

Shifting Mindsets

Shifting mindsets for a successful redesign requires a deep commitment to change. Remember, change takes time, and it is essential to remain patient, listen to our people, and be persistent throughout the process.

CHAPTER 11

Visionary Leadership for Business Transformation

To be clear, when I'm talking about the type of leaders who are going to need significant development to make this transformation a success, you know I don't mean you, right? You're reading this book; I already know that you're exactly the right person to steer this ship. Leaders are readers! But it's those other leaders that I'm thinking about, those are the ones that we might need to influence to have the right mindset, ideology, qualities, and desire for development.

Those in leadership positions have got to where they are because they either founded the company, worked their way up by demonstrating exceptional skill in their field, or are adept at motivating and leading teams. Or maybe their uncle was the CEO. But it is an unreasonable expectation for all leaders to have the same skills, or to be an expert in every emerging technology, or to already know how to lead an AI-first company into the future. This chapter will advise you on leadership qualities that will influence a successful transformation, and there are some leaders who may need to take an introspective look at their leadership style or areas for development. Just as you'd expect from your employees as we navigate these changes.

The Leadership Role as Project Sponsor

The project sponsor plays a critical role in driving the success of automation and AI initiatives. The project sponsor should hail from the executive c-suite for an organization-wide transformation or be the most senior person responsible for the business function leading the change. The project sponsor sets the tone for the entire project and should have a leadership style that is collaborative and consults on decision making with the technology experts in the project team. This individual should be an inspirational and influential figure who needs to provide guidance, resources, and support to project teams. The project sponsor acts as a liaison between the project team and the rest of the organization, ensuring alignment, evangelizing about the benefits, managing expectations, and removing any obstacles that may hinder progress.

Leaders must demonstrate their commitment to cognitive technologies by allocating sufficient resources, setting ambitious and strategic goals, and actively participating in the transformation process. They should clearly define responsibilities and communicate them to their teams to ensure everyone is aligned, motivated, and working toward a common goal.

As we mature, we should also have sponsors for advancing the technology. For example, leadership could appoint sponsors who are experts in AI or machine learning to oversee the adoption of these technologies within their respective areas. These sponsors act as advocates, mentors, and facilitators, ensuring that the organization maximizes the benefits of the technology throughout each function and prepares use cases for the future as the technology advances.

Leadership Development

We discussed in Chapter 9 how our L&D teams can provide leadership development in the areas of change management, executive coaching, and emotional intelligence. But to take this further, we need to see leadership development as an ongoing process that requires a continuous commitment to learning and growth. Visionary leaders prioritize not only their team's requirement to upskill but also ensure their own personal development is viewed with the same magnitude. They actively seek out learning opportunities, such as workshops, seminars, and mentorship programs, to stay updated on emerging trends and technologies. By sharing their own development journey and goals openly, leaders can inspire their teams to embrace change and strive for excellence.

In today's era of advancing cognitive computing capabilities, leaders must possess a solid understanding of these technologies. Technology education programs equip leaders with the knowledge and skills needed to make informed decisions, assess new technologies, and effectively communicate with technical teams. Such education empowers leaders to advance the digital landscape and harness automation and AI opportunities for driving innovation and productivity.

Leaders can benefit from tapping into the expertise of external mentors and experts in the intelligent automation arena. These individuals offer valuable insights, share best practices, and provide guidance on navigating the challenges and opportunities of the digital age. I would advise you to pair leaders with mentors or consultants who have already successfully led organizations through digital transformations, facilitating knowledge exchange, support, and personal growth.

Qualities of Inspirational Leadership

The technology is going to keep advancing, our transformational redesign is going to need continual strategic reviews, and our people need to remain motivated and committed throughout the change. This puts the pressure on leaders to develop an inspiring leadership approach that aligns with the challenges and opportunities posed by automation and AI.

Let's explore how visionary leaders can tackle this challenge:

- **Embracing a digital mindset**
  - Leaders must embrace a digital mindset that acknowledges technological advancements and harnesses their transformative impact. This involves adapting to change, maintaining a technically skilled workforce, and championing ways of working using technology and trending practices. Leaders need to demonstrate and advocate for assessing emerging technologies and understanding their applications within the organization.
- **Visibility, inspiration, and personal connection**
  - Inspirational leadership hinges on being visible, approachable, and inspiring to teams. Leaders should cultivate genuine

connections with employees, demonstrating a vested interest in their well-being and professional growth, particularly crucial for remote, distributed teams where face-to-face interactions may be limited. Consider publishing diaries, regular video updates, and social media updates to keep the organization in touch with the activities of senior leadership and continue the narrative of our progress toward the organizational goals.

- **Servant leadership and empowerment**
  - Leaders should adopt a servant leader mindset that emphasizes the importance of trusting the expertise of their team members and providing a culture and environment that gives them what they need to get things done. By focusing on serving the needs of their team members first, leaders empower them to embrace new technologies, take calculated risks, and innovate. This dedication to the well-being of the team demonstrates that trust in your experts can result in increased motivation, better collaboration, and superior performance.

- **Cultivating a growth mindset**
  - A growth mindset is crucial for leaders in the age of automation and AI. They must embrace challenges, seek continuous improvement, and view failures as invaluable learning opportunities. Leaders need to encourage experimentation and calculated risk-taking, to enhance innovation, autonomy, and resilience. Good leaders involve teams in decision making, communicate goals and expectations clearly, and be active in addressing concerns to facilitate hyperautomation.

- **Transparency, feedback, and ratings**
  - Effective leadership means being open to feedback and actively seeking it out, whether it's from their direct reports or colleagues at all levels. By listening to what employees have to say, being vulnerable and honest about feedback received, leaders can build trust and confidence within the

organization. This approach can keep employees motivated and engaged, knowing that their input is valued and
considered. Performance reviews should not be just about
evaluating the employees below you—it's important to
use feedback to enhance leadership skills too and ensure
everyone is working towards a common goal.

- **Thought leadership**
  - o Leaders have an incredible opportunity to showcase their
    expertise and share innovative ideas with a global audi-
    ence through social media platforms and external events.
    By regularly posting insightful content, thought-provoking
    articles, and success stories, leaders can establish themselves
    as trusted voices in their industry and with their employees.
    This not only boosts their personal brand but also enhances
    the reputation of the organization they represent. Consider
    collaborating with industry influencers, other executives, and
    intelligent automation experts to amplify efforts to becom-
    ing an automation-first organization. Visionary leaders will
    leverage social media and speaking appearances effectively,
    inspire others, spark meaningful conversations, and drive
    positive change in their respective fields.

- **Aligning automation with business objectives**
  - o Leaders should ensure that hyperautomation initiatives are
    tightly aligned with the strategic objectives of the organiza-
    tion. They need to steer their teams to identify transforma-
    tional, high-impact projects and prioritize them accordingly.
    Leaders need to take a keen interest in the results, data,
    and key performance indicators that track the impact
    of automation on critical business metrics. In doing so,
    visionary leaders make data-driven decisions that further
    steer the organization toward sustained success on the
    automation-first roadmap.

- **Leading with purpose and shared values**
  - o Leading with purpose involves aligning actions not only
    with the organization's digital transformation vision but also

with the culture and agreed-upon values of the business. Leaders need to openly demonstrate these principles and celebrate team members who exemplify admired values, creating a sense of unity and ownership among employees. Through consistent reinforcement of shared values and purpose-driven leadership, organizations can cultivate a strong, meaningful culture that drives success.

- **Collaborative decision making**
  - Progressive leaders exhibit adaptability in decision making and push against wanting every approval to land on their desk. They understand the importance of collaboration and cross-functional teamwork and that good decisions come from trusting your teams. Leaders should actively seek input from diverse perspectives, enable interdisciplinary collaboration, and promote a culture of collective ownership, recognizing that innovation often stems from the synergy of different expertise and viewpoints.

- **Ethical and trusted leadership**
  - Inspirational leaders prioritize ethical considerations in their decision making and actions. They uphold integrity, transparency, and accountability, ensuring that business goals are pursued ethically and responsibly. This inspires trust and confidence among stakeholders and embodies integrity and social responsibility within the organization.

- **Resiliency and responding to challenges**
  - Leaders need to remain steadfast in their commitment to organizational goals, contextualizing setbacks, and failures as learning opportunities and embracing change as a catalyst for growth. They are adept at swiftly altering strategies, reacting to new information, and embracing innovative solutions that address emerging challenges and opportunities. They need to be an example to others by having the ability to navigate ambiguity and lead with confidence to inspire resilience and perseverance among team members, driving success even in challenging circumstances.

- **Commitment to human-centric values**
  - ○ Leaders will need to take tough decisions when navigating an organizational redesign; however, considerations need to be made to ensure AI's impact on jobs will be limited. While certain processes may be automated, the instinct should be for most jobs to experience augmentation rather than replacement. Forward-thinking leaders should collaborate with governments and institutions to enact policies that support human capital, offering upskilling and reskilling opportunities first, embracing the value-added activities that only human ingenuity can offer, and facilitating a supported, seamless transition for displaced workers where necessary.

Valuing People and Profit

So, who can we look to as examples of visionary leadership? Let's focus on the leaders and organizations who prioritize innovation through technology, and who lead business growth and profitability at the same time as valuing employee voices, empowerment, and experience.

Chuck Robbins, CEO of Cisco, is a great example of valuing inclusivity and innovation. He proactively addressed racial inequities within Cisco, leading a swift 100-day plan to tackle the issues and positioning the company ahead of societal shifts on racism. During the COVID-19 pandemic, Robbins prioritized customer needs over profits, offering flexible financing and enhancing Webex capabilities to support remote work.[1] Under his leadership, Cisco has been recognized as the #1 company on the World's Best Workplaces™ list, with 98 percent of employees rating it as a great place to work.[2]

Reshma Saujani, as the founder of Girls Who Code, empowers young girls, particularly from under-represented backgrounds, to pursue careers in technology, essential to creating a more inclusive and innovative industry and society. Her leadership philosophy encourages taking risks and learning from failures. Her leadership style emphasizes mentorship and networking,[3] showing how it's our people that drive organizational transformation.

Susan Wojcicki, the prior CEO of YouTube, embodies a commitment to innovation, integrity, and inclusivity. She transformed YouTube into a profitable entity by embracing changing customer needs such as mobile viewing and personalized online advertising. She prioritizes a diverse and inclusive workplace, which drives both employee satisfaction and organizational success. The ability to align ambitious business goals without compromising strong ethical standards is a great example of visionary leadership.[4]

Ginni Rometty, former CEO of IBM, led IBM's expansion into cloud computing, AI, and quantum computing, showing how even a century-old company needs to stay relevant amid technological advances. Rometty's push for hiring based on capabilities rather than academic credentials echoes our ideas on the importance of a skills-based workforce that values diversity and employability. "Bosses, she argues, should encourage staff to build skills that keep them and their employers relevant in the marketplace."[5]

Jensen Huang, CEO of Nvidia, utilizes the flat organizational structure we explored, believing it to be the most empowering model. He emphasizes trust in his team's abilities and expertise, granting them autonomy instead of giving conventional top-down instruction. Huang encourages real-time feedback from his team and champions radical transparency, making meetings open to all employees and sharing strategic directions openly. Nvidia's approach has delivered both exceptional profitability and return on investment as well as attracting top talent in the technology sector.[6]

How AI Will Change Leadership Roles

Automation and AI will fundamentally reshape the role of leaders.

These technologies offer leaders unprecedented opportunities to optimize operational efficiency and reallocate their focus strategically. By delegating their own routine tasks to intelligent systems, leaders can dedicate more time and effort to driving innovation and accelerating long-term growth.

As automation tools and AI algorithms mature, leaders will rely on AI-driven insights to inform decision-making processes and adapt strategies accordingly. By harnessing AI-powered analytics, leaders can get insights into complex business challenges, enabling informed decision making and strategic planning. AI-driven insights provide leaders with a strategic advantage in navigating uncertain market conditions, identifying emerging opportunities, and mitigating risks. As AI technologies evolve, leaders will have more access to quality data, more sophisticated tools for scenario planning, predictive forecasting, and risk management, empowering them to steer their organizations toward sustainable growth and profitability.

Looking ahead to the next decade or two, the role of leaders in mature and advanced AI-first organizations will undergo profound transformations driven by emerging technologies. Leaders will adapt to using cutting-edge cognitive technologies, such as advanced AI, but then further shifts can be made by combining this with augmented reality and virtual reality, which will enhance the user interfaces, making data and models come alive in 3D, accelerating decision-making capabilities that drive innovation. (I know you're picturing the computer screens in the film Minority Report, so am I!) These technologies will enable leaders to immerse themselves in virtual environments for real-time collaboration, strategic planning, and talent development, regardless of geographical barriers. Augmented decision-making interfaces could provide leaders with personalized insights and recommendations, leveraging machine learning algorithms to anticipate market trends, consumer preferences, and competitive dynamics.

The time will come when leaders integrate personal AI assistants and coaches into their daily routines, leveraging these intelligent systems to enhance productivity, facilitate knowledge acquisition, and provide proactive support in decision-making processes. These AI assistants will analyze vast amounts of data, identify patterns, and generate actionable recommendations tailored to each leader's unique preferences and objectives. Advances in natural language processing and conversational

AI will enable leaders to utilize human–machine interactions to create a partnership of cognitive computing and their own business acumen, customized to their knowledge, style, experience, and industry.

As AI reshapes the business world, visionary leaders must embrace responsible automation practices and prioritize creating value through intelligent automation. By understanding the impact of AI on jobs, supporting employees, and investing in the core elements of AI, leaders can navigate the AI revolution successfully and drive meaningful change for businesses as well as society. Leaders of the future will be examining how AI can be used for good, ensuring responsible and equitable deployment of these technologies.

As technology continues to advance exponentially, the role of leaders will evolve beyond the traditional role of today, embracing an approach that combines technological advances with human-centric leadership principles.

CHAPTER 12

AI-Driven Decision Making

Data Visualization

Data is king and should be a core part of your transformation programs. Ensure you have a dedicated role or team to take ownership of this and deploy a strategy that gives both people and AI the access to real-time data that will influence decision making and analytics.

Unless your data are protected by privacy laws, or can be commercially sensitive if made public, then you should not have any barriers to anyone accessing any data in your organization. I'd recommend a central data hub, which articulates your strategy and how it aligns with the values and goals of the organization. The hub should provide one source of access to raw data, key performance metrics, and visual, business intelligence dashboards for all areas of the organization. If I work in warehousing and I want to see supply chain demand data, I should not have to request access via an IT ticket, I should be able to navigate to the data I need. I'd also recommend the data be displayed in central areas in physical workplaces to make access to the data easy and simple.

A data visualization strategy has the following benefits:

- People are informed and engaged in the company's health and performance.
- People are able to form opinions, ideas, and insights based on simple, intuitive, storytelling-based visuals of the data.
- People are able to access data to submit their ideas for automating processes.
- People are able to consider continuous improvement by understanding the as-is.
- People are able to make better informed, evidence-based decisions.

- People can trust the single source of quality data to have confidence in their actions and decisions.
- People are able to use one source of data for consensus, collaboration, and cross-functional problem-solving.
- AI is able to use the data for
  - advanced analytics;
  - adding context;
  - unearthing additional insights;
  - suggesting ideas actions, and strategies;
  - predictive modeling;
  - anomaly detection;
  - recommending or automating decisions;
  - removing administrative burden from human roles.

AI-Driven Decision Making

In our AI and automation-first organization, we are going to implement AI-driven decision making to sustain our digital success. We can use AI to understand vast, complex data sets, and we can use machine learning to continually learn from the data and adapt accordingly. Power this with digital twin technology and we have a safe space to experiment with our AI-driven ideas to test the predicted impact and results.

AI-driven decision making can take various forms:

Assisted: AI can be used to analyze data to provide results, but the human still looks at the data and makes the decisions. This could be, for example, a health care professional using AI in diagnostics; their specialism and experience still trump AI knowledge, but they will benefit from the acceleration of AI to get through the amount of data required to make the decision.

Augmented: AI could analyze large amounts of historical data and make recommendations based on its knowledge of a market and the patterns or trends indicated in the data, which is then passed to a human to make an informed decision. Consider how financial traders could make investment decisions in this way.

Table 12.1 Types of AI-driven decisions

	Monitors	Informs	Recommends	Decides
Assisted		AI		Human
Augmented			AI	Human
Automated	Human			AI

Automated: AI, machine learning, and RPA can combine to analyze and learn from the data and decide to take action based on how the model has been trained, or how decisions have been programmed to be executed in an automation. A human would simply monitor and own the process. This could have use cases in supply chain management or customer service requests as an example (Table 12.1).

Case Studies

Let's have a look at some real-life examples....

Sloan Kettering Cancer Center is using AI from IBM Watson to analyze tens and thousands of medical records, treatments, and outcomes associated with individual patients. Given data on a new patient, Watson looks for information on those with similar symptoms, as well as the treatments that have been the most successful. The idea is it will give doctors a range of possible diagnoses and treatment options, each with an associated level of confidence. The result will be a system that its creators say can suggest nuanced treatment plans that take into account factors like drug interactions and a patient's medical history.[1]

Ant Financial leverages AI to handle all critical decision-making tasks, including loan approvals, financial advice, and authorization of expenses. This automation allows Ant Financial to efficiently manage over a billion customers, scale rapidly, enhance operational efficiency, and seamlessly integrate various business functions, which gives them a competitive edge in the financial services industry.[2]

Salesforce uses its internal AI system, Einstein, to enhance decision making and provide unbiased forecasts, modeling, and analysis based on data from Salesforce applications. During staff meetings, Einstein listens to executive updates and offers insights on various business aspects, identifies strengths and weaknesses, and even flags specific inaccuracies or bias or internal politics that may need attention. This data-driven approach ensures transparency and objectivity and aids decision-making processes by relying on AI's impartial analysis.[3]

The Mayo Clinic has harnessed digital twin technology to enhance diagnostics and treatment through patient-specific models. By integrating different data sources such as medical imaging, genetic information, and wearable devices, the clinic creates digital twins that simulate a patient's physiology. This aids decision making by enabling physicians to deeply understand their patients' conditions and design risk-reduced targeted treatment plans. By analyzing these digital twins, doctors can explore various treatment options, predict intervention effectiveness, and optimize patient outcomes in a safer way. [4]

Decision Making for an Automation Pipeline

We covered in our shifting mindsets chapter about incentivizing employees to suggest ideas for using AI and automation, we need people to not feel threatened by parts of their existing role being automated, but to feel excited about the impact it could have on the organization, and the impact a successful idea could have both on their career success and on their bonus. But access to the data is key here too.

When submitting an automation idea, the data are imperative to be able to conduct a thorough and detailed assessment considering factors such as the associated costs, potential benefits, relevant metrics, and alignment with organizational goals. We can use AI or manual calculation to estimate what the benefits will be once automated and a thorough representation of this will help get buy-in from the stakeholders to understand the feasibility and the impact and select it for automation. This informed assessment is key to making strategic decisions regarding automation.

We should then prioritize our pipeline based on a range of criteria, from the estimated benefits, the capability of the team, the complexity and length of time to implement, the expected cost or time savings, and many others that will need to be decided on by your governance council and weighted in accordance with organizational strategy. This approach ensures that your efforts are directed toward areas where they can yield the most significant impact and contribute the most to your transformative redesign.

During the decision-making process for what to automate, and in what use cases we can deploy AI, we must ensure we can establish mechanisms for monitoring their performance and realizing the anticipated benefits over time. The strategy and methods have to be agreed upon before selecting the process for automation. This should entail defining the key performance indicators, what success looks like, how AI can be used for monitoring, a commitment to regularly evaluate and measure the results, and timepoints agreed to utilize the data for continuous improvement purposes.

Impact on Digital Transformation

AI-driven decision making provides organizations with the unparalleled capacity and precision needed to proactively propel the organization forward. By using AI, we can gain a deeper understanding of what influences our performance the most, we can transform the way we measure, analyze, and align performance, we can replace outdated, static metrics with dynamic, intelligent, real-time analytics, and we can provide a more comprehensive insight into the organization's operations and future opportunities.

By making data transparent and readily accessible, we encourage the right culture for digital transformation that values data-driven discussions among teams. By providing a clear view of our performance to all audiences, we establish a single source of truth that helps individuals understand our current position and the actions that need to be taken.

Having an agreed approach to AI-driven decision making paves the way for more informed and effective business strategies.

CHAPTER 13

Managing Risks and Ensuring Sustainable Change

I'm afraid I never get excited by risk management, but I know it's necessary when approaching any change, especially one as transformational as organizational redesign.

But if you're not excited either, before you groan and skip forward to the next chapter, please humor me for a moment, risk can actually be a really positive thing! Having worked on technology adoption projects for all of my career, I've learned (and not the easy way let me assure you) that risk isn't the delivery blocker we quite often see it to be. Risk keeps us safe and helps us keep the auditors satisfied if we approach this with the right mindset.

Without risk where would our lessons learnt come from? And therefore, how do we take those lessons and apply them to future change? With risks and risk management comes growth and isn't that what we are all here trying to achieve?

So, if you're still with me, I'm going to make this chapter helpful and insightful, so you approach risk management from a new perspective, helping you ensure your change is sustainable.

De-Risking Our Innovation

The technology we've discussed can help us better identify, assess, and mitigate potential risks. Predictive analytics, AI, and machine learning can provide data-driven insights, enabling us to be proactive with potential issues. Simulation tools and digital twins allow organizations to experiment in a virtual environment, reducing the risks of innovation by allowing for safe trial and error. Robotic Process Automation (RPA) significantly contributes to compliance, audit, and regulatory adherence by automating tasks that result in improved accuracy in data handling, reduced human error, and a comprehensive audit trail.

Combine this use of technology with some of the other concepts we've discussed such as iterative development that can identify and address risks as we build, process re-engineering where we can design our processes with a focus on eliminating or reducing risk, and a continuous improvement ethos meaning we can be adaptable as we encounter and mitigate risks. This approach not only creates a resilient risk management strategy but means we can be comfortable with our appetite to take calculated risks.

Risk Appetite and Risk Tolerance

Risk appetite reflects how comfortable an organization is with the potential risk of making changes to the ways of working, products, and other initiatives they are driving. The gauge of their willingness to handle uncertainty in pursuit of success. Risk appetite is an organization's capacity to deal with risks. It sets a boundary, indicating the maximum level of risk that is deemed acceptable, even after various safety measures are put in place.

On the other hand, risk tolerance is about how much scope they have within that boundary. Perhaps saying, "We're ok with this much risk, but only up to a certain point, especially when it comes to achieving the end goal."

Businesses use their risk appetite to figure out if they're taking on the right amount of risk while going after their objectives. Typically, all this is laid out in a written document, so everyone in the organization knows where they stand and the role they play.

Factors that shape risk appetite, which plays a huge part in managing risks in a business, can come from various sources, including:

- The organization's culture.
- The organization's industry.

- The organization's competitors.
- Types of initiatives the organization pursues.
- The organization's current industry position and financial strength.
- The organization's reputation.

However, how much risk you're willing to tolerate can change from one situation to another. It all depends on things like the type of project you're working on, how long it's supposed to take, and the expertise of the team involved.

Plus, risk tolerance isn't set in stone. It can shift over time as industry rules, regulations, and what's considered normal change. So, what might be an acceptable risk today could be totally different down to the road (Figure 13.1).

Knowing about the organization's risk appetite and tolerance gives us an idea of what is acceptable and how we can manage this and mitigate what is not. Keep this quote in mind, "If you fail to plan, you are planning to fail." This same sentiment applies when it comes to successful risk mitigation planning.

The only way for effective risk reduction is for an organization to use a step-by-step risk mitigation plan to sort and manage risk, ensuring the organization has a continuity plan in place for unexpected events.

Risk mitigation involves crafting a strategy to either reduce the impact or eliminate risks that a business might face. Once the organization has developed and implemented that strategy, it's vital for them to

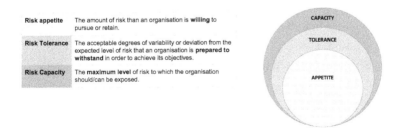

Source: Elaborated by the authors based on various sources including the Institute of Risk Management and Business continuity Institute

Figure 13.1 Risk tolerance[1]

monitor progress and be prepared to adjust as the business grows and evolves over time.

While risks differ significantly across industries, there are several commonly recognized risks that generally impact the majority of organizations:

Compliance risk: When an organization breaches both internal and external regulations, it threatens its reputation and financial stability.

Legal risk: This refers to a compliance risk where the organization violates government regulations, leading to potential financial and reputational harm.

Operational risk: This happens when the organization faces potential losses in its regular operations because of unsuccessful or flawed processes.

Risk Mitigation Strategy

Now we have a handle on risk types and what risk mitigation is, we just need the stepping stones to create a robust risk mitigation strategy. This strategy should carefully consider the impact of each risk and prioritize them according to severity.

Below are some common risk mitigation strategies often used together, depending on the specific business risks and how they might affect the organization.

Risk acceptance: Sometimes, it's worth embracing a risk if the potential rewards outweigh the possible downsides. This doesn't have to be a permanent decision, but for a certain period, it might be the best move, especially when dealing with more serious risks and threats.

Risk avoidance: When we opt for risk avoidance, we're actively taking steps to steer clear of potential risks. This approach might mean making sacrifices in other areas or adjusting our strategies to minimize the chances of encountering those risks.

Risk monitoring: After analyzing and identifying risks, organizations often choose to actively keep an eye on them. This doesn't mean eliminating the risks entirely; rather, it involves accepting that they exist and taking measures to limit potential losses and prevent them from spiraling out of control. AI and machine learning can be used to monitor risks and alert us to when attention is needed.

Risk transfer: There are instances where it's practical to transfer the risk to someone else. This might mean handing over the risk to a third party, like an insurance company. For instance, when organizations buy insurance policies, they can offload the risk of property damage or personal injury onto the insurer, which helps minimize their own financial vulnerabilities.

Organizations evolve, and so do their needs. That's why it's crucial to have solid metrics for tracking each risk, its category, and the corresponding mitigation strategy over time. A good approach might be scheduling weekly meetings to discuss risks or using AI algorithms to track any changes in the risk profile.

Reporting

The final step in the risk mitigation strategy is to put the plan into action and then reassess it based on monitoring and metrics to see how effective it is. There's a constant need to evaluate and tweak it as needed.

The Risk of Being Risk Averse

We discussed in detail the risks of changing and we've talked about how best to accept, avoid or mitigate risk; but we haven't taken a look at the other side of risk....

What's the risk of NOT changing??

We think so much about the risks associated with change, but we need to really consider and weigh those risks up against playing it safe and not looking to see if the grass is greener on the side of change.

So, say we play it safe, and we don't change, what's the risks associated here, and why being risk averse to change isn't always the *play it safe* option? We are aware of the obvious outcomes of not changing, loss of customers, loss of revenue, redundancy, losing the competitive edge in the market. This then becomes a huge black hole that becomes harder and harder for organizations to dig themselves out of.

But what about all the other red flags that happen before this because the old familiar security blanket feels much safer than the unknown? These are actually things that can happen way before the demise and could give you early warning that the risks of not changing far outweigh remaining the same and stable.

Here are some of those early warning signs.

Loss of Your Reputation and Influence in Your Industry

Not keeping up with changes can really impact how much influence and respect an organization has in its industry. In today's ever-evolving business world, if you're not moving forward, you're falling behind compared to competitors who are innovating and transforming to meet the demands of the market.

If organizations resist change, they end up outdated, losing market share, and losing influence in the industry. So, it's vital for businesses to stay flexible and update their strategies to stay competitive and keep their good name intact.

Staff Retention

When organizations refuse to change, they often end up losing staff for a variety of reasons. For starters, employees want the opportunity to grow and work in a dynamic setting, one that provides them with the scope for progression.

If a company stays stuck in a rut, there's not much room for people to develop personally or professionally, which can lead to them feeling frustrated and disconnected. Satisfied employees want to be part of the solution and help their organizations innovate. When leadership resists change, it sends a message that they're not really thinking ahead or open to new ideas, which can push talented employees to look for places where their skills and potential are appreciated. And in industries that are always changing, employees might feel like sticking with a company that's not moving forward is holding them back in their careers. Loss of top performers really has a detrimental impact on culture and employee sentiment.

Product Development

If you're not embracing change, your product development could hit a wall. When you're not innovating or adapting, customers might lose interest and start looking for better options elsewhere. That means they won't be willing to spend money on your product if it's not giving them what they need. It's crucial to stay in tune with industry trends, user expectations, and new technologies. Otherwise, you risk creating products that just don't match up with what people want anymore. And that puts your company's relevance and profitability on the line. Basically, keeping up with what customers want and how the market is changing is the key to staying successful in today's competitive landscape.

These are all risks that provide you with the early warning signs that you need to change before the irrecoverable risks take hold of the organization and it becomes too late to change. Think of these like the symptoms you sometimes overlook because you don't want to bother the doctor, or you're worried about the outcome … listen to what your organization is telling you.

Sustainable Change

We need to move with the times and we know where there's change, there's risk associated. How do we make sustainable and, where possible, risk-averse change? Let me be clear, you're never going to achieve change that's completely risk-free, but we can make change sustainable enough to at least try to mitigate risk as much as possible.

Creating lasting change within an organization involves several key tactics.

First off, it's all about keeping everyone in the loop. Organizational leadership teams need to be upfront about why changes are happening, what they hope to achieve, and how it all fits into the big picture. When everyone understands the why behind the changes, it's easier to get everyone on board.

Involving employees in the decision-making process and listening to their feedback helps build trust and makes them feel like they're part of the solution. Plus, giving ownership of change back to employees helps with having the full picture of what could be impacted both positively and negatively. Employees are on the front line building relationships with customers and suppliers, they understand trends and the impacts so they will know how a change can impact day-to-day operations and therefore will speak up if it's going to put the organization at potential risk.

Next, it's crucial to support employees through the transition. That means providing the right tools, training, and resources they need to adapt. Whether it's offering workshops or one-on-one coaching, giving employees the support they need helps them feel confident in their ability to handle the changes. Recognizing and celebrating progress along the way is also key. Small wins can boost morale and keep everyone motivated to keep pushing forward. If your employees feel threatened, confused, or unsupported then they can pose one of the biggest risks to the change and the organization overall. Supporting the employees is vital to risk mitigation and therefore sustainable change. We know how we personally feel when something changes and we have no control over it, so why do this to the organization's employees?

Lastly, change should be seen as an ongoing process, not a one-time event. Encouraging a culture of continuous improvement means being open to new ideas, learning from mistakes, and always looking for ways to do things better.

We've adapted a model from the Project Management Institute, and believe this gives sound guidance on how to approach sustainable change in a hyperautomation organization (Figure 13.2).

When you make sustainable changes, you're not just being cautious, you're strengthening your ability to handle risks and to always be ready. By encouraging adaptability and resilience in your team, you're preparing your organization to face challenges head-on. In today's

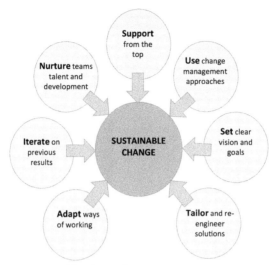

Figure 13.2 Sustainable change[2]

fast-paced business world, this proactive approach isn't just helpful—it's necessary for lasting success.

CHAPTER 14

The Impact of Intelligent Organizations

There is understandably a lot of conversation, fear, and trepidation surrounding the impact of AI and automation on the world. From concerns about job displacement to the use of deepfakes and misinformation, and even fears of potential world domination, the discourse around AI and automation often veers toward the extreme. While some of these concerns may be exaggerated or sensationalized in the media and films, there are indeed still real threats that we face. As we continue to integrate AI and automation into our businesses, societies, and economies, making responsible, ethical, and people-centric policies an absolute priority becomes imperative.

With the development of generative AI, comes the increased risk of exploitation by malicious actors who could leverage AI-generated content for nefarious purposes, such as deepfakes, which can deceive and manipulate the public, or be used as humiliation such as the case with revenge porn. To address this, robust regulations governing AI development and deployment must be implemented, ensuring transparency, accountability, and adherence to ethical AI practices. In addition, there needs to be legal ramifications and consequences for such use.

The European Union has recently passed the EU AI Act, with the aim of creating a trustworthy, legal framework for AI to operate in by ensuring that AI systems respect fundamental rights, safety, and ethical principles and by addressing risks of very powerful and impactful AI models. This will mean transparency is required on why AI made certain decisions or providing obligations to developers and deployers of AI to conform to standards or even avoid high-risk use cases.[1] I expect more such regulations to come.

Even for those of us using generative AI for nonmalicious purposes, we should be obligated to disclose if we are using AI-generated content, images, or videos, and not pass it off as a human creation or portrayal. Similarly, if you use AI voices or chatbots in your customer services, which is fine if you're adding value, the recipient should be made aware of who they are conversing with.

Building media literacy, educating people on critical thinking, and developing verification tools are crucial for evaluating synthetic media but we also need to be transparent and accountable for our use of AI to preserve trust in our work.

Another pressing issue is job displacement and income inequality resulting from automation-driven job loss. As AI automates more tasks, certain jobs could become obsolete, which left unaddressed would lead to unemployment and economic instability. It's essential for the workforce to adapt to new roles and for policy makers to implement strategies to mitigate the impact of automation on employment. And this isn't a future of work thing, this is a now thing, policies are needed to ensure organizations do not instigate mass layoffs without first redeploying or reskilling staff, otherwise, the consequences for the wider economy can be dire. Responsible organizations can use this technology to drive profitability and innovation, unethical organizations who seek to use this technology to replace the workforce in favor of profit will do so at the detriment of the economy, which will affect their bottom line in the long term anyway.

Algorithmic bias and privacy violations are also critical concerns. AI systems learn from historical data, which if you've ever been on the internet, you'll realize probably already contains biases, so this will perpetuate discrimination if left unchecked. For example, research shows that women currently make up less than 26 percent of the AI workforce,[2] that's a future problem for us all if there's a risk of unconscious bias in AI systems.[3] So, bear that in mind when you're critically evaluating AI outputs, and if you are in a position of influence, advocate for women to join the industry or your teams.

I hope I've convinced you that AI and automation offer enormous benefits for your organization, but it's clear on a global level that we must advance with caution. Vigilance, ethical practices, and global cooperation are paramount to ensuring that our AI-driven future remains safe, secure, and equitable for all. It's imperative that governments and policy makers around the world collaborate on fit-for-purpose regulations and policies to address these issues.

> "Responsible AI isn't just a moral imperative; it's a strategic necessity for organisations navigating the complexities—and the benefits—of an AI system. As you embrace the transformative power of AI, do so with a commitment to responsible innovation, ensuring that technology serves as a force for good in our interconnected world."[4] SS&C Blue Prism

I believe we need a collective, global agreement on people-centric policies and the will and intention to use AI and automation for the good of humanity. Artificial intelligence and robotics can do things so much faster than all of us, and put to the right uses, we could see huge leaps forward in creating a better world for all.

And I am an eternal optimist, so let's have a little look at what that better world could look like....

The Impact of Intelligent Automation on the Organization

Intelligent automation can be a transformative force for organizations, delivering benefits that will enhance profitability and drive growth. That's true without having to displace a single human worker.

- By automating routine or time-consuming tasks, businesses can unleash the full potential of their people, redirecting human efforts toward strategic or creative endeavors and innovative initiatives.

"Using intelligent automation, an organization can increase productivity and efficiency, improve the customer experience, lower costs, and make better decisions faster. The goal is not to replace human experts but to free up their time for the kinds of strategic and nuanced activities that help grow the business."[5] Jeff Erickson, Tech Content Strategist, Oracle

- Through advanced AI and machine learning capabilities, businesses can analyze vast troves of data, gaining deep insights into customer behaviors and preferences. This enables them to anticipate customer needs and deliver highly personalized services, which should lead to enhanced loyalty and a competitive edge in the market.

"The playing field is poised to become a lot more competitive, and businesses that don't deploy AI and data to help them innovate in everything they do will be at a disadvantage."[6] Paul Daugherty, Chief Technology and Innovation Officer, Accenture

- Deploying intelligent automation will give organizations a huge advantage to decrease costs, increase revenue, enhance profitability, and free up resources that you can do more and better things with.

"In labor-intensive sectors, such as wholesale and retail, AI augments the human workforce, enabling people to become more productive, leading to a profit increase of almost 60 percent. In capital-intensive industries such as manufacturing, AI powered machines will eliminate faulty machines and idle equipment, delivering constantly rising rates of return, resulting in equally dramatic profit increases of 39 percent by 2035. Regardless of industry, companies now have a significant opportunity to apply

> **AI and invent new business capabilities for growth, profitability, and sustainability."**[7] Accenture

- The future of offices and the widespread adoption of remote work represents a strategic opportunity for businesses to thrive in a digital world. By embracing intelligent automation and remote or hybrid work practices, organizations can enhance their agility, efficiency, and competitiveness, positioning themselves for sustained success.
- Intelligent automation supports remote collaboration by providing tools and technology that facilitate communication, project management, and workflow automation.

> **"As we continue to integrate AI into our remote work practices, we're not just changing how we work; we're redefining the very nature of work itself. The future of AI and remote work is bright, and it's ours to shape and optimize for the betterment of all remote workers."**[8] Virtual Vocations

- Remote work enabled by automation reduces overhead costs associated with maintaining physical office spaces. By leveraging intelligent automation technologies that support remote operations, businesses can streamline administrative tasks, optimize resources, and minimize the need for expensive office infrastructure. This translates into significant cost savings, improved financial health, and competitiveness in the market.
- Intelligent automation can play a crucial role in enabling remote work by automating critical processes, securing data, and maintaining productivity levels across distributed teams.

> **"The industry has been moving towards integrated intelligent automation where AI-enabled workflows fit seamlessly into the larger process paradigm. As (organisations) strategically deploy automation within existing workflows to offload manual tasks,**

(Continued)

(Continued)

> **employees can look forward to a rewarding hybrid workplace that values their time and effort."**[9] Babu Sivadasan, Chief Executive Officer, Jiffy.ai

- In the realm of investment, intelligent automation can play a pivotal role in attracting funding and driving growth. Startups that embrace intelligent automation differentiate themselves by showcasing their ability to leverage cutting-edge technologies for efficiency and productivity gains as well as retaining their funding for key spending such as research and development rather than administrative staff or tasks.
- Investors are drawn to startups with a clear advantage over their peers, especially those capable of disrupting traditional business models through AI or automation-driven innovation.

> **"With intelligent automation, early-stage startups have process efficiencies right out of the gate."**[10] Concetta Yates, Vice President Customer Strategy, SS&C Blue Prism

- Environmental sustainability is another area where intelligent automation can provide benefits for organizations. By optimizing resource utilization, reducing waste, and enabling more efficient processes, it contributes to a greener and more sustainable business. Organizations can hit their green targets and a reduced environmental footprint while still achieving significant cost savings.

A business that adopts AI and automation will reap the rewards of increased efficiency, innovation, productivity, profitability, and competitive advantage.

Impact on Economies

As organizations thrive, so do economies, and, in turn, as economies thrive that leads to a more favorable environment for businesses to operate in.

- Reports show that the adoption of intelligent automation could have a profound impact on GDP growth, with estimates it could be 14 percent higher by 2030 as a result of AI, adding $15.7 trillion to the global economy.[11]
- Healthy economies fuel innovation, job creation, and increased consumer spending, to the benefit of organizations and society.
- Intelligent automation enhances labor productivity by automating repetitive and time-consuming tasks, which allows for more work to be completed at a quicker pace than before. As a result, organizations can achieve higher output with the same or fewer resources, leading to benefits for the organization as well as increased GDP growth.

> **"Labor productivity growth, a key driver of economic growth, has slowed in many economies…. AI and automation have the potential to reverse that decline: productivity growth could potentially reach 2 percent annually over the next decade, with 60 percent of this increase from digital opportunities."**[12] McKinsey Global Institute

- Automation eliminates manual errors, reduces operational costs, and accelerates processes meaning businesses can achieve cost savings and improve overall efficiency. These savings can then be reinvested in innovation, research and development, and other growth initiatives, further stimulating GDP growth.
- By automating processes, businesses can deliver products and services more efficiently, reduce time to market, and offer competitive pricing. This allows organisations to capture a larger

market share, attract investments, and contribute to growing the economy.

> **"AI algorithms can be used to analyze and predict global economic trends, allowing businesses to make more informed decisions and maximize their global market share."**[13] Daniela Haluza, University of Vienna

Organizations need to think long term about the economy when considering decisions around replacing workers with AI and automation. If too many workers lose their jobs, or incomes do not rise to reflect the increased profitability gains from automation, then economies will stagnate, consumerism will fall,[14] and inequality, crime, and poverty could rise.

We should also remember that robots do not pay tax, and robots do not spend money in our businesses, people do, keeping an active workforce who contribute taxes and have disposable income is essential for economies to operate successfully. Organizations who want to operate in a thriving economy need to carefully enact policies that utilize the technology, but also prioritize the job security of employees and the health of the economy.

Impact on Politics and Government

We need our policy makers to move forward with progressive and enabling policies for AI and automation, to support changes to education, and to set the right conditions for businesses to utilize this technology. But if there was ever an area where we could benefit from automation speeding up processes then it has to be this one right? And I'm sure that's true no matter where in the world you are reading this.

- AI and automation have the potential to revolutionize government and politics, by delivering improvements in efficiency, transparency, and citizen engagement.

> "In order for AI technologies to be truly transformative in a positive way, we need a set of ethical norms, standards and practical methodologies to ensure that we use AI responsibly and to the benefit of humanity."[15] Susan Etlinger, Industry Analyst, Altimeter Group

- AI could analyze policies, laws, bills, and regulations and examine them in accordance with the views and opinions of engaged citizens.
- AI can be used to predict the impact of political decisions and propose amendments.
- AI algorithms could facilitate consensus-building, identify common ground, and reduce partisan gridlock, leading to more effective governance.
- AI has the potential to transform political campaigns by tailoring messages to individual voters, delivering personalized campaign content based on their unique preferences and concerns. This could increase voter engagement, voter turnout, and provide a deeper understanding of political manifestos.
- AI-powered fact-checking could be deployed during political debates and speeches to provide real-time corrections, reducing the spread of misinformation, and promoting informed decision making. (We're sure you won't find it too difficult to think of a political figure who this would be useful for.)
- In addition to enhancing political processes, automation can streamline national and local government operations with the goal of improving citizen experiences. Public sector departments can use automation to increase productivity to enable them to still meet the needs of constituents even with shrinking budgets.
- By automating processes, government administrations can save operational hours and costs, allowing employees to focus on higher-value tasks, such as decision making, innovation, and delivering projects that can enhance the lives of the public.

- AI-powered analytics can anticipate citizens' needs and canvas requirements or opinions, enabling governments to proactively address issues and maintain transparency and trust.

> **"As technologies evolve, policymakers, advocates, and citizens will need to keep up to ensure AI is leveraged as a force for a better and more inclusive democracy."**[16] Brookings Institution

By embedding intelligent automation into government operations, we can make governments more agile, responsive, and citizen-focused, ultimately enhancing governance and democracy.

Impact on Education

Developing education for AI and automation, and indeed digital skills in general, is essential to provide us with the skilled workers that the future needs, as well as equip us with the necessary cognitive abilities to navigate the world AI will create.

And it's not just technical skills, the importance of soft skills, such as influencing, negotiation, leadership, empathy, creativity, problem-solving, take on an increased credence when we are sharing the work between artificial and human intelligence.

- In schools, AI has the potential to revolutionize traditional curriculums by offering personalized learning experiences tailored to individual student needs.
- AI can assess aptitude levels and adapt content difficulty to match students' intellectual capabilities or neurodiversity needs, creating a more engaging and effective learning environment.
- AI-powered tools can assist teachers by augmenting instructional techniques or by the use of interactive content, providing valuable insights into student progress and performance.
- Automation can free up teachers from time-consuming administrative duties, allowing them to focus on the work that matters the most.

- AI can deliver virtual tutoring that can provide the personal assistance and attention that may not always be possible in large class sizes.

> **"It'll enable every student in the United States, and eventually on the planet, to effectively have a world-class personal tutor."**[17] Sal Khan, Khan Academy

- Educational institutions, and employers, can leverage AI and automation to provide automated content in accordance with curriculum or preferences. The 'Netflix of Learning' as we often hear.
- Machine learning and AI algorithms could be used to detect plagiarism or provide personalised feedback, correction, or recommendations.

Side note: I look back fondly on Microsoft Clippy who used to pop up in the 1990s and early 2000s when we were in Microsoft Word saying, "it looks like you are writing a letter...." Now think of AI as a superpowered Clippy who can pop up and say, "It looks like you are writing code...." and then offer specific coaching recommendations to help you complete it accurately. See, everything comes back into fashion again eventually!

- AI-driven technologies can enable higher education facilities to develop smart classrooms with virtual tutors, fast access to research and analytical tools, and real-time feedback, enhancing the overall learning experience.

> **"Our hope is that the advent of AI will spur educators, students, parents, and policymakers to come together to consider what skills our students really need to navigate uncertainty, solve complex challenges, and shape meaningful futures in a changing economy."**[18] World Economic Forum

- In adult education and employee professional development, AI and automation can facilitate continuous lifelong learning by automating and enhancing training and development programs. Employees receive personalised learning experiences tailored to their specific needs and career goals, driving skill development.
- The move to automation requires a culture of learning within organisations, motivating employees to explore new technologies and acquire diverse skill sets to adapt to evolving job requirements.
- Provision of digital skills education is imperative to provide employees with job security as new skills are gained, enabling them to stay in the workforce.

> "AI innovations such as natural language processing, artificial neural networks, and robots can improve L&D process efficiency, evaluate learning aptitude, and track learning progress."[19]
> European Journal of Training & Development

Education systems need to redesign themselves to fit the requirements of future students and workers and promote a culture of lifelong learning. By leveraging these technologies, policy makers, educators, and employers can empower individuals to thrive in our rapidly advancing world.

Impact on Jobs

As more and more tasks and functions are automated, and as technology continues to advance, the nature of all jobs will change, and no business will remain untouched. They say all businesses are digital businesses now.

When the conversation turns to AI replacing us, I like to remind people that artificial intelligence may be faster, but it does not have your unique opinions, expertise, or experience. That cannot be replaced and there will always be a need for humans to work. Besides, we want to work; we want to have value, belonging, and worth, which are innate human needs. But we do need to adapt to embrace the technology that will change the jobs we know today.

> **"We will adapt to these changes by inventing entirely new types of work, and by taking advantage of uniquely human capabilities."**[20] Pew Research Center

This book advocates for a collaborative workforce of humans and computers working collaboratively to achieve strategic outcomes, with humans and AI workers focusing on what they do best, and redesigned processes for seamless interaction.

> **"We will need new hybrid-skilled knowledge workers who can operate in jobs that have never needed to exist before. We'll need farmers who know how to work with big data sets. Oncologists trained as roboticists. Biologists trained as electrical engineers. We won't need to prepare our workforce just once, with a few changes to the curriculum. As AI matures, we will need a responsive workforce, capable of adapting to new processes, systems, and tools every few years."**[21] Amy Webb, Founder, Future Today Institute

- Humans bring creativity, empathy, and critical thinking to the role, and machines excel at repetitive and data-intensive tasks. Teams and processes need to be redesigned to accommodate the strengths of both.
- Some jobs will be phased out in most organizations, such as administrative duties, data entry, or bookkeeping, for example, yet it will still need humans to oversee and own that business process. Humans will still need to ensure the work is done, to communicate the results to other stakeholders, or to implement changes or improvements in how the robots execute the tasks.

- More jobs will be created with demand rising for skills we've talked about in this book such as machine learning, robotics, data science, cyber security, or AI specialists for example.[22]
- Skilled manual jobs are at less of a risk from replacement. We will always need those expensive plumbers; yet technology will change how they execute the work with robot assistance, advances in power tools, or AI-enabled sensors or monitoring, for example. Digital skills will be required by all of us.

> **"My greatest hope for human-machine/AI collaboration constitutes a moral and ethical renaissance—we adopt a moonshot mentality and lock arms to prepare for the accelerations coming at us."** [23] Barry Chudakov, Founder Sertain Research

- For a lot of the work, it will still need humans to monitor the work of machines, for example, AI can process thousands of diagnostics images of cancer scans, or a backlog of DNA samples to be tested for the police. Yet the more complex or ambiguous cases should rightfully be referred to a human to apply their expertise and nuanced experience. Those skills are still needed but we will thankfully have AI to process the routine tasks in a way that can accelerate the work and leave skilled professionals to prioritize where they spend their time.

> **"AI's ability to augment human capabilities rather than replace them enables collaboration and opens doors to new opportunities."** [24] Soumyajit Chakraborty, CEO, SoftProdigy

- Intelligent automation will enhance human potential by automating routine tasks, allowing employees to focus on work that requires human skills and judgement. This augmentation will not only enhance productivity but will also contribute to job satisfaction and drive more specialisation in a chosen field.

- Intelligent automation will reduce the cognitive load on employees by automating repetitive, mundane work and routine decision-making, enabling people to focus on higher-level thinking, problem-solving, and utilising data to form insights and strategies. This will lead to reduced stress and better-informed decision-making.

> **"Organizations that use machines merely to displace workers through automation will miss the full potential of AI. Such a strategy is misguided from the get-go. Tomorrow's leaders will instead be those that embrace collaborative intelligence, transforming their operations, their markets, their industries, and—no less important—their workforces."**[25] Harvard Business Review

Humans will always have a future in the workforce and have irreplaceable qualities; when we redesign our organization, we need to put the skill development of our people as a priority and augment their roles to be complemented by the vast benefits and acceleration of AI and automation.

Impact on Employee Experience

The integration of AI and automation into the workplace can bring significant positive changes in employee experience and the concept of work itself.

- By automating repetitive and mundane tasks, employees can focus on more strategic and value-added activities, leading to higher job satisfaction, developing new skills, experiencing fulfillment, and contributing to their personal and professional growth.

> **"Technology will free us from day-to-day drudgery, and allow us to define our relationship with "work" in a more positive and socially beneficial way."**[26] Pew Research

- Productivity gains can be used to deliver a better work-life balance by reducing the need for long hours and manual effort. With automation handling time-consuming tasks, employees can have more control over their time, allowing them to prioritise personal commitments, embark on further learning opportunities, or spending more quality time with their families.
- Flexible working arrangements supported by automation can also be used by organizations to support employee well-being, positive mental health, or removing the barriers to work that may be experienced by parents or carers.
- Just as in the last industrial revolution there was the push to reduce the burden of work to a 40-hour workweek, this fourth industrial revolution allows us to consider a shorter workweek yet again, with no productivity lost through the use of automation.
- The transition from a traditional 40-hour workweek to a four-day workweek has been shown to improve productivity, reduce stress, reduce absenteeism, improve physical and mental health, and allow employees to experience a greater quality of life[27], which leads to happier workers driving positive outcomes for your business.

> **"When employees feel more in control of their work-life balance, they get more engaged and grow more loyal to the company they work for."**[28] Adriana Cacoveanu, Yarooms

- Remote work facilitated by automation allows companies to access skills and expertise from a global talent pool, promoting diversity and cultural exchange within the organization.

- Flexibility in work arrangements, as well as the people-centric environment this book advocates for, not only attracts top talent but also provides a more inclusive work environment.
- With intelligent automation-driven productivity gains, organizations and nations are able to re-evaluate the concept of work itself, and how much each of us should need to work to earn a living wage.

> **"With some of the biggest companies in the world now moving to a hybrid or 100% remote working model, the need for flexibility and adaptability is crucial to retain and attract the best talent."**[29]
> Roboyo

- AI can be used to support talent development strategies such as career coaching, or tailored performance support, to provide globally distributed teams the development they need to progress in their careers.
- Intelligent automation can be used to survey, analyze, and ultimately improve employee engagement levels.
- AI-driven analysis can help inform decision making on salaries, rewards, and benefits and provide evidence or consensus for the proposals.

> **"Everyone will have access to amazing AI. Your creative talent though—that will be who you are. Instead of chasing that race to the bottom on labour costs, invest in turning your talent into a team of explorers who can solve amazing problems using AI as the tool that takes the busy work out. That is the company that wins in the end."** Vivienne Ming, Cofounder, Socos Labs

The future of work holds promise for greater productivity, innovation, and output for organizations, yet also offers us the unique opportunity to reinvent the concept of work, deliver a positive employee experience, and enable a more enjoyable work and home life.

Impact on the Planet and Quality of Life

When we have that collective agreement to use AI for good, and the investment and resources to make it happen, we can use the ability of intelligent automation to process data at an accelerated pace to present solutions to improve our planet and our quality of life.

- With the increase in productivity, the use of AI for education, and the job creation of new roles, we have the opportunity to reduce income inequality and more fairly redistribute wealth.
- With a focus on enabling individuals to upskill, more people could transition into higher-paying jobs.

"Those countries that have AI technology will be much better off and will be able to create new value if AI is used as a means to improve rather than undermine the wellbeing of citizens."[30]
ScienceDirect Journal

- We're already seeing advances in this area but using intelligent automation for health care could lead to improved quality of life and increased life expectancy.

"The evidence suggests that artificial intelligence holds great promise for improving global health outcomes through enhanced research capabilities, improved clinical decision-making, better tailored care plans, automated administrative tasks, and reduced costs associated with inefficient resource allocation throughout the healthcare system."[31] Daniel Haluza, Medical University of Vienna

---

- With AI-powered diagnostics, we can provide faster diagnosis, better access to care, and more personalized treatment options.
- Precision medicine powered by AI algorithms can tailor treatments, leading to increased life expectancy and better management of chronic illnesses.

"I think it is more likely than not that we will use this power to make the world a better place. For instance, we can virtually eliminate global poverty, massively reduce disease, and provide better education to almost everyone on the planet."[32] Erik Brynjolfsson, Director, MIT Initiative on the Digital Economy

- AI and computer vision can be used to help in the global effort to identify criminals, prevent sexual trafficking, and identify child abuse victims, among other opportunities to prevent harm to people.

"We set a goal of helping the national center for missing and exploited children to use AI to accelerate the coordinated national response from 30 days to 24 hours after reports of abuse. In order to accomplish this goal we needed to create custom algorithms to recommend where in the world an image was likely accessed to accelerate coordination with the right law enforcement agency. Machines were able to do the tedious repetitive work and humans were freed up to do the investigation and analysis that made the reports actionable to recover victims."[33] Lisa Thee, AI Thought Leader and Author

- Consider the effects of intelligent automation on climate change to accelerate research, hypothesize solutions, or more rapidly develop innovations.
- We can use the technology for environmental sustainability by optimizing resource utilization, reducing waste, and enabling more efficient processes.
- Renewable energy sources and AI-optimized energy grids could reduce carbon emissions.

"By utilizing the power of AI, we can develop strategies to reduce emissions and develop more efficient ways to produce energy and other essential resources. AI can also help us make better decisions about the use of energy resources and help us protect our environment from the impacts of climate change."[34] Daniel Haluza, Medical University of Vienna

- The predictive powers of AI and machine learning could help us better predict weather patterns or natural disasters, or automate early warning systems to enhance our responses.
- Farming could use predictive analytics and automated machinery to increase crop yields or innovate solutions to reduce the environmental impact.
- Conservationists could use AI to accelerate research or to use AI-powered drones to monitor wildlife areas, detect signs of poaching, or track endangered species.
- Let's put AI in front of telescopes to continue the work of surveying galaxies, identifying new planets, or have AI piloting exploratory spacecraft to expand our knowledge of the universe.
- We could have smart cities with AI assisting urban planning initiatives to prioritize green spaces or innovate for efficient public transportation.

"AI can be used to analyze data from various sources and identify patterns that can help to make cities more efficient, reduce crime, and improve public services."[35] Daniel Haluza, Medical University of Vienna

- AI could analyze historical data and use predictive analytics to predict crime hotspots and suggest solutions, or allocate resources for proactive prevention.
- AI can be used to help public safety and provide accurate information in the event of another global pandemic.

"In the early days of the pandemic.... We realized that one of the most valuable things we could offer is a trusted advisor about the crisis. The result was a chatbot that pulled live data from the CDC and the World Health Organization to answer questions about the COVID-19 virus. By tracking the most common answers and linking to the most up-to-date information from reliable sources, we made our little contribution to the world in a time of crisis. Engaging with a chatbot feels like a conversation because it is. We gave thousands of users valuable information and a bit of comfort in a time of terror."[36] Maggie Meacham, Author of AI in Talent Development

- AI can be used for real-time language translation, not only enhancing communication in global workplaces but also contributing to global unity by erasing language barriers in diplomacy or trading.

"AI in language translation is more than just code; it's a bridge connecting people from diverse backgrounds. As technology advances, so does our capacity to break down barriers, fostering a more interconnected world."[37] Serin Noman, AI Monks.io

Putting my pessimistic hat back on for a moment, AI-driven data centers do significantly increase energy and water consumption, leading to potential environmental harm, which we cannot ignore. We need to offset this with a global focus on using AI for good, prioritize solutions for advanced cooling systems, as well as using it to accelerate the push toward renewable energy being our primary source of energy provision.

As technology continues to evolve, the potential for AI and automation to create a better world for future generations is limitless, providing we have that will and intention to use it for the good of humanity and the planet.

Impact on Society

AI adoption gives us the power to use productivity gains to create a society where everyone can thrive, and where happiness, not just profit, is an indicator of a country's success.

> **"If elements of community happiness are part of AI objective functions, then AI could catalyze an explosion of happiness."**[38] Greg Shannon, Chief Scientist, Carnegie Mellon University.

- By handling time-consuming administrative tasks, automation allows individuals to focus on innovative ideas and business ventures, adding to global advances and output.
- With the reduction in working hours or a provision of a universal basic income, we create opportunities for entrepreneurship which will drive economic growth but also create a more inclusive society where anyone can pursue their passions.
- By freeing individuals from repetitive and mundane work, automation could enable people to engage in more meaningful and fulfilling work, bringing higher job satisfaction, increased motivation, and greater happiness in the workforce.

> **"Automation is the gift of time. It's an opportunity for people in many different roles to use their time differently to create more value. It's an opportunity to dramatically unlock the power of labor to focus on what matters most."**[39] Mike Gilfix, VP, IBM Automation

- If we change the concept of work and bring in programmes to offset the displacement of workers, such as, again, reduced working hours or a universal basic income, we can give value to the necessary but often unpaid work such as volunteering, caring, parenting, or community engagement.

- We could see an increase in arts and culture as the time gained back could be used to dedicate more time to learning new skills or engaging in artistic activities.
- Consider the Covid-19 pandemic where many non-essential workers had more time; how many people do you remember engaging in new hobbies, learning new skills, and spending time helping others in their community? We could have this again, without the health crisis.

> "Why try to push everyone into paid work, if you can objectively see that there are not enough jobs around? Why not give people who have good alternatives the opportunity to reduce work, or not work at all, and cash in the basic income? 'Good alternatives' include the opportunity to upskill or retrain. It's also possible that the (universal basic income) policy could redefine what society has historically considered work. Caregivers—predominantly women—could be remunerated for traditionally unpaid labour, such as raising children or caring for elderly relatives." [40]
> Loek Groot, Associate Professor of Economics, Utrecht University

- Reducing barriers to work is another potential benefit of our new world. By providing flexibility in terms of working hours and location, we enable individuals, especially women, parents, and carers, to pursue professional careers whilst still able to complete personal commitments.
- AI and cognitive technology supports and enables concepts such as flexible working, remote working, or a reduced working week. This can deliver more inclusivity and diversity in the workforce and a more equitable society where everyone has the opportunity to participate and contribute and where everyone shares in the benefits of this technology.
- Universal Basic Income should be seriously considered as a potential solution to the challenges presented by automation. By providing every citizen with a regular, unconditional sum of money from the government, we ensure that individuals have

a basic level of income to cover their needs—offsetting any negative effects of displaced workers or fewer jobs in a particular industry or location.

- AI and Chatbots can be used to provide citizens with advice on personal finances, debts, access to benefits, or budgeting advice with a goal of decreasing financial stress and enhancing education in this area.

"**We must do away with the absolutely specious notion that everybody has to earn a living. It is a fact today that one in ten thousand of us can make a technological breakthrough capable of supporting all the rest. That is a fact, and it then begs the question, how do we make sure we invest in every single one of those people such that all of society maximizes its collective ROI?**"[41] Scott Santens, Evonomics

---

- Universal Basic Income should be seriously considered as a potential solution to the challenges presented by automation. By providing every citizen with a regular, unconditional sum of money from the government, we ensure that individuals have a basic level of income to cover their needs – offsetting any negative effects of displaced workers or fewer jobs in a particular industry or location.
- Trials have shown participants are more likely to continue education, seek more fulfilling or higher paid work, engage in community work or business ideas, as well as evidence it reduces poverty and improves health. All these benefits for the individual would result in a positive effect on the economy, and thus businesses too.[42]

"**A UBI policy in response to AI and automation would address the failure of employers to distribute the spoils of economic growth—propelled, at least in part, by automation – fairly among**

workers."[43] Karl Widerquist, Professor of Philosophy, Georgetown University-Qatar

- We can use AI to support minorities or marginalised communities by providing access to digital education, healthcare services, and economic opportunities, to ensure the advances in technology benefits all people and could create a more equitable world.
- AI and chatbots can be used to provide citizens with advice on personal finances, debts, access to benefits, or budgeting advice with a goal of decreasing financial stress and enhancing education in this area.
- AI can be used to measure and monitor the wellbeing and happiness of citizens, with analytics to recommend further courses of action. The world could be measured by a global happiness index, and not just by an increase in GDP.

"I strongly believe the answer depends on whether we can shift our economic systems toward prioritizing radical human improvement and staunching the trend toward human irrelevance in the face of AI. I don't mean just jobs; I mean true, existential irrelevance, which is the end result of not prioritizing human well-being and cognition."[44] Bryan Johnson, Founder and CEO, Kernel

AI and automation have the power to transform society and enhance the happiness of people in profound ways. If we have that collective agreement to use the advancement of technology to better our world, we can build a future where technology and humans work together to create a happier and more prosperous society for all.

"We can build and use technology that is peaceful in its intent, serves the public good and is rooted in societal trust. It is possible but only through a deep intention by those building it, principled

leadership by those tasked with regulating it, and active participation from those of us experiencing it."[45] Verity Harding, Author of *AI Needs You*

CHAPTER 15

Rebuilding the Future of Work

And here we are at the final chapter, I hope my passion for sharing my experiences and ideas on technology, AI, automation, and organizational redesign has resonated with you. But more than that, I hope you've connected with my desire to change our world for the better.

Let's recap why we need to rebuild the way our organizations work —and, most importantly, what's in it for us. After all, disruption is meaningless without a driving force behind it.

Efficiency and Productivity

Enhanced process efficiency naturally boosts productivity and revenue, delivering positive impacts to your bottom line. A streamlined workplace empowers employees to focus on value-adding tasks and skill development. By eliminating waste and inefficiencies, organizations gain the momentum needed to drive sustainable growth.

Adaptability and Innovation

Embracing change creates a culture of adaptability and innovation. When employees are encouraged to think creatively and act autonomously, continuous improvement becomes second nature. By leveraging employee insights and giving time back to employees to allow human ingenuity to thrive, companies gain a motivated workforce with continuously evolving skills.

Employee Experience and Satisfaction

When employees are happy, they are your best ambassadors. Involving employees in the change and redesign process strengthens their sense of ownership and commitment. Technology projects should be delivered with the business, not to the business, and the outcomes should make work more fulfilling. Remember it's people who will make the change a success, technology only enables it.

Customer Satisfaction and Retention

Happy employees lead to happy customers. Streamlining processes, eliminating bureaucracy, and focusing on meaningful human interactions improve customer relationships. Simplifying the way customers interact with your business gives you a competitive edge, making it easier for them to choose you over your competitors.

Organizational Reputation

A culture that champions innovation, combined with efficient processes, creates a more enjoyable and productive workplace. This, in turn, boosts service quality and strengthens your industry reputation. Word of mouth is a powerful tool, and a positive reputation builds loyalty and trust. To maintain these advantages, ensure your organization remains agile, continuously evolving in line with emerging technology and future of work best practices.

Key Takeaways

1. **Nothing is off the table** when innovating. Be open to all possibilities and experiment freely, because every experience—whether a success or a lesson learned—brings valuable knowledge. True innovation requires challenging the status quo, imagining every possible use case, and exploring every avenue.

REBUILDING THE FUTURE OF WORK   235

2. **Involve everyone**: Organizational redesign is a collective effort. Employees need a seat at the table and must fully buy into the vision. When they are part of the process, they take ownership and are accountable for delivering the vision.

3. **Design for human–AI collaboration**. When redesigning work and processes, ensure that human and AI collaboration is embedded into every facet of the business. AI should not replace human contributions but enhance them, creating opportunities for employees to leverage their creativity, problem-solving skills, and emotional intelligence.

4. **Stay current**: Don't get left behind—keep up with emerging technology and understand its role in your organization. Be transparent with your employees, alleviating their fears and helping them see the benefits of new tools and processes.

5. **Modernize your culture**: Redesigning processes is not enough— culture must change alongside it. If you don't align your culture with your new ways of working, all the hard work will fall flat. Shift mindsets, and make sure your culture supports the continuous change.

6. **Leadership needs to be bold**: Leaders must not only guide from the top down but also be willing to modernize their own style and make their own development visible and inspirational. Organizational redesign comes with risks, but playing it too safe can stifle real transformation. Collaborate with risk and compliance teams to push the boundaries while protecting the business.

7. **Have a vision**: You need a north star to follow, this will not succeed without strategic aspirations and a vision to keep you on the right path. It needs to be both realistic and achievable, but also exciting for what the future could bring. This always reminds me of a part in the book *Alice in Wonderland* written by Lewis Carroll....

> One day Alice came to a fork in the road and saw a Cheshire cat in a tree.
>
> *"Which road do I take?"* she asked.

> *His response was a question: "Where do you want to go?"*
> *"I don't know," Alice answered.*
> *"Then" said the cat, "it doesn't matter."*

Without a clear and inspiring vision, your transformation will lack direction.

Human Connection

Another last thought to leave you with is the value of humans and human connection. We've discussed how we need to be careful to not see automation and AI just as a means to replace human jobs. It's an opportunity to give more time to creating meaningful human interaction.

Remember in your organization that the value of the time you have saved by deploying AI or automating processes shouldn't be viewed simply in monetary terms, but in what your people can do instead with the time you have freed up; what added value can they bring, what business development, improvements, client relationships, or creative endeavors can they work on instead with that gift of time. The role of humans is in guiding, supervising, and complementing the technology to achieve optimal outcomes for the organization.

When your organization becomes more innovative, agile, and efficient, what can you do with that to help the world, your people, your community, or to advance the services and products you provide? The human element remains central, and AI should improve, not replace, that connection.

Also, think about your end user preferences. How many people do you know who actively avoid supermarket self-checkouts because they still want to converse with a human and to avoid those human jobs being lost? Think about those times when as a consumer you have struggled to speak to a customer service person and not a robot, and how the majority of us have all experienced that frustration and the damage that does to the reputation of the customer service industry. Imagine you create content, perhaps educational or social media videos, do you want your end users rolling their eyes at the proliferation of AI videos you're now using, and longing for the days of real people and human-to-human interaction? AI and automation should be focused on making our employee and customer experiences better in a way that feels like progress.

Humans and AI: The Future of Work

What does the new world look like? Remember in chapter one the example of what a day in the office could look like in the future? I realize that could be super aspirational for you right now, or maybe it isn't. What is important to remember is that while examples of other organization's journeys are aspirational and inspiring, that is *their* journey into transformation. Transformation and redesign are a unique and tailored journey, and therefore don't be put off or overwhelmed by some of the large-scale use cases and examples, do what works for you, just be sure you use the approaches and techniques outlined here. Because I know this works!

I promise you that by following the steps in this book to implement AI and automation, you will make more money. I promise you that your organization will thrive. It's not a bad thing to want this.

But wouldn't it be wonderful to realize those benefits while simultaneously changing the world? As a leader, you have an unprecedented opportunity to be part of a movement that can change the lives of workers forever. To use the productivity gains of AI and automation to enable people to work differently, work less, work smarter. We can give people the gift of time to spend on themselves, with their families, helping their community, on the arts, hobbies, learning new skills, or entrepreneurship. If we all have that societal goodwill and intention to use it to solve the world's problems, to provide equal opportunity for all of society to reap the benefits of these advances, then we could see some real progress in the world. Together, we can turn this vision into reality, using AI as a force for both business success and social progress.

Thank you for coming on this journey with me. I hope you're now motivated and at least a little more passionate about shaking up the stale corporate rut that organizations find themselves in. It's time to take these learnings, rip up that rule book, and redesign your new world.

Please ensure you review the extra resources outlined in the next section for you as you don't have to just take my word for it, there's a wealth of knowledge and examples out there waiting for you. I'm sure you can also teach me a thing or two and I'd love to hear from you to continue this conversation.

As we close this chapter and this book, remember people remain the heart and engine of our organization.

Let's create a world where AI and automation are seen as an opportunity to make a difference. It's time to redesign our reality, rebuild the future of work, and revolutionize the way we live.

Further Reading

I'd recommend you continue your journey by reading the following excellent books.

Adamson, J. 2024. *Geeks with Empathy*. rJeremyAdamson.com

Barkin, I., Bornet, P., & Wirtz, J. (2020). *Intelligent Automation: Learn how to harness Artificial Intelligence to boost business & make our world more human.* World Scientific Publishing.

Burnett, Sarah. 2022. *The Autonomous Enterprise: Powered by AI*. British Computer Society.

Davenport, T. H., Barkin, I., & Davenport, C. (2024). *All Hands on Tech: The AI-Powered Citizen Revolution*. Wiley.

Harding, Verity. 2024. *AI Needs You: How We Can Save AI's Future and Save Our Own*. Princeton University Press.

Hindle, John, Lacity, Mary C., and Willcocks, Leslie. 2019. *Becoming Strategic With Robotic Process Automation*. SB Publishing.

Hindle, John, Smith, John, Stanton, Matt, and Willcocks, Leslie. 2024. '*Maximizing Value With Automation and Digital Transformation: A Realist's Guide*. Spinger Link Publishing.

How, Neil. 2018. *Run Fast: The Definitive Guide to Accelerating Technology Projects*. Rethink Press.

Leifer, L., M. Lewrick, and P. Link. 2018. *The Design Thinking Playbook: Mindful Digital Transformation of Teams, Products, Services, Businesses and Ecosystems*. Wiley.

Mather, Jayne. 2023. *Super User Networks for Software Projects: Best Practices in Training and Change Management*. British Computer Society.

Meacham, Maggie. 2020. *AI in Talent Development: Capitalize on the AI Revolution to Transform the Way You Work, Learn, and Live*. Associate for Talent Development.

Minnaar, Joost. 2019. *Make Work Fun*. Corporate Rebels.

Rosenberg, A. 2019. *Science Fiction: A Starship for Enterprise Innovation*. Kindle

Santens, Scott. 2021. *Let There Be Money: Understanding Modern Monetary Theory and Basic Income*. Independent.

Spohrer, J. 2022. *Service in the AI Era: Science, Logic, and Architecture Perspectives*. Business Expert Press.

Winder, P. 2020. *Reinforcement Learning: Industrial Applications of Intelligent Agents*. O'Reilly Press

West, Darrell M. 2018. *The Future of Work: Robots, AI, and Automation*. Brookings Institution.

Further Reading

Glossary

Acronym	Term	Description
	4th Industrial Revolution	The ongoing transformation of traditional industries through the adoption of smart technologies and digital solutions.
	5G Networks	5th generation of wireless mobile/cellular technology giving faster data speeds.
	Agile Principles	Flexible work practices emphasizing continuous improvement and adaptability to meet evolving business needs, guided by principles such as those outlined in the Agile Manifesto.
	AI Assistant	A virtual assistant powered by artificial intelligence algorithms that can perform tasks such as scheduling meetings, answering emails, and providing relevant information based on user input.
	AI-Driven Decision Making	The use of artificial intelligence (AI) to analyze vast and complex datasets, generate insights, and make informed decisions. AI-driven decision making can take various forms, including assisted, augmented, and automated decision making.
API	Application Programming Interface	An API is a type of programming code designed as a way for two or more computer programs to interact or exchange information with each other.
AI	Artificial Intelligence	Software that mimics human intelligence and thinking. It encompasses algorithms and systems that can learn from data, recognize patterns, and make decisions with minimal human intervention.
AR	Augmented Reality	A technology that overlays digital information or virtual objects onto the real world, enhancing the user's perception and interaction with their environment.
	Automation Maturity	The level of advancement an organization has achieved in implementing automation technologies, ranging from initial exploration and experimentation to full-scale integration and optimization.

(continued)

Acronym	Term	Description
	Autonomous Vehicles	Vehicles equipped with advanced sensors, navigation systems, and artificial intelligence algorithms that enable them to operate and navigate without human intervention
	Benchmarking	Comparing organizational performance metrics against industry standards or best practices, identifying areas where the organization lags behind and opportunities for improvement through re-engineering.
CoE	Center of Excellence	The key team in the organization that play a pivotal role in the delivery of the intelligent automation program by driving the adoption, best practice standards, and methods for success
	Change Agents	Individuals designated to champion the change initiative within their respective areas of the organization are tasked with educating, engaging, and supporting their colleagues through the change process to drive successful implementation.
CIA	Change Impact Analysis	An assessment of the potential impacts of a change on various aspects of the organization, including people, processes, policies, and systems, aimed at understanding the magnitude of change and planning appropriate interventions to mitigate risks and challenges.
	Chatbot	A chatbot is a computer program that simulates a conversation with human users, typically through text-based or voice-based interfaces.
CHIN	Chin Model	The CHIN model helps assess and respond to challenges during organizational change by considering control, help, influence, and noise factors.
	Citizen Developer	An employee who is not part of the central IT or CoE team but is trained and empowered to create and manage automations as needed.
	Cloud Virtualization	The virtualization of computing resources, such as servers, storage, and networks, that are delivered as services over the internet from cloud service providers.

(continued)

Acronym	Term	Description
	Cognitive Technology	Computer systems that emulate human cognitive abilities and thought processes, enabling tasks like data analysis and decision making through artificial intelligence and other advanced techniques.
	Collaborative Workforce	Collaborative workforce refers to human and digital co-workers working within the same team on the same processes in unison.
	Computer Vision	AI that enables computers to interpret and understand the visual world through digital images or videos, mimicking human vision capabilities such as object recognition, scene understanding, and image analysis.
	Continuous Improvement	Regularly evaluating and enhancing processes, products, and services to drive ongoing enhancements and efficiencies
	Culture	Organizational culture is the shared values, beliefs, and behaviors that define how people work together.
	Customer Journey Mapping	Mapping out the customer's interactions and experiences throughout their journey with the organization, highlighting pain points and areas for improvement to enhance the overall customer experience.
CRM	Customer Relationship Management	Software applications designed to help businesses manage interactions with current and potential customers, streamline sales and marketing processes, and improve customer service and satisfaction.
	Data Analytics	Utilizing data analysis techniques to identify patterns, trends, and areas of inefficiency in business processes, guiding re-engineering efforts toward areas with the most potential for improvement.
	Data Governance	The framework of policies, procedures, and controls that ensure the quality, integrity, security, and availability of data across an organization, while also ensuring compliance with regulations and standards.
	Data Strategy	A comprehensive strategy focusing on data visualization, analytics, security, and governance to enable AI-driven insights.

(continued)

Acronym	Term	Description
	Data-Driven Decision Making	Data-driven decision making relies on factual insights from organizational data to inform decision-making processes, driving continuous improvement and adaptability.
	Deep Learning	Deep learning is designed to mimic the structure of the human brain, the neural networks. Deep learning describes how a computer can learn about a topic using the addition of complex data and without human intervention
	Design Thinking	Design thinking is a problem-solving method that emphasizes empathy, creativity, and collaboration. It helps organizations develop innovative solutions by understanding and addressing the needs of stakeholders.
	Digital co-worker (Also referred to as Virtual Colleague or Software Robot throughout this text)	Software robots that work alongside people to automate and transform business processes, performing tasks in your systems following a process, step-by-step, at the keystroke level.
	Digital Infrastructure	The technological foundation comprising cloud-based platforms and technologies to support AI and automation deployment.
	Digital Transformation	Strategically integrating digital technologies and solutions to modernize, improve, and advance your organization
	Digital Twin	A virtual replica or simulation of a physical asset, process, or system, which enables real-time monitoring, analysis, and optimization of its performance and behavior.
DEI	Diversity, Ethics, and Inclusion	Creating an inclusive environment that embraces diversity and ethical principles, ensuring equal opportunities for all employees, and integrating ethical considerations into policies and procedures related to automation and AI.
	Edge Computing	Edge computing means data processing occurs closer to the data source or "edge" of the network, rather than in centralized data centers, allowing for faster data processing
	Emotional Intelligence	The ability to recognize, understand, and manage one's own emotions, as well as to perceive and influence the emotions of others, which is crucial for effective leadership, teamwork, and interpersonal relationships in the workplace.

(continued)

Acronym	Term	Description
	Employee Experience	Prioritizing the well-being and engagement of employees in the workplace for organizational success.
ERP	Enterprise Resource Planning	Integrated software systems that manage core business processes, such as finance, human resources, and supply chain, in a unified and centralized manner.
	Future of Work	Concepts, trends, and predictions shaping the evolution of the workplace, workforce, and work methods.
	Gap Analysis	Compares the current state of the organization with its desired future state in terms of readiness and strategic alignment, identifying areas for improvement.
Gen AI	Generative AI	Artificial intelligence systems that can create new content, such as images, text, or music, based on patterns and data it has been trained on.
	Governance Council	A governing group of key stakeholders at an organization responsible for overseeing automation initiatives, defining policies, and ensuring alignment with organizational objectives.
	Human Connection	Meaningful relationships and interactions between people that contribute to a positive experience and feelings of well-being
	Human-Centric Automation	Human-centric automation emphasizes designing automation solutions that complement human capabilities rather than replacing them.
	Human-Centric Manifesto	A formal declaration outlining the organization's commitment to prioritizing people, promoting a collaborative workforce, and emphasizing that automation is meant to enhance, not replace, human workers.
	Human–Machine Collaboration	The partnership and interaction between humans and digital co-workers to accomplish tasks, combining the strengths of both to achieve optimal outcomes.
	Human-in-the-Loop	A step or steps in an AI or automated process where human oversight, input, or intervention is incorporated into the decision-making process or workflow.

(*continued*)

Acronym	Term	Description
HMI	Human–Machine Interface	The point of interaction between humans and machines, typically in the form of user interfaces, controls, or displays, that allows users to communicate, control, and receive feedback from digital systems or devices.
	Hyperautomation	Hyperautomation is the concept of utilizing intelligent automation for the purpose of automating everything in an organization that can be automated.
IA	Intelligent Automation	Intelligent automation takes the "doing" from RPA and combines it with the "learning" from ML and the "thinking" from AI technology.
	Leadership Development	The ongoing process of enhancing leadership skills and capabilities through continuous learning, growth, and personal development initiatives.
ML	Machine Learning	AI that enables a system to learn and improve its own performance by continuously incorporating new data into an existing model, or developing new behaviors based on experience, patterns, and rules.
NLC	Natural Language Classification	Natural language classification enables digital co-workers to learn organization- or industry-specific language so that they understand the context and can respond accordingly.
NLC	Natural Language Generation	Natural language generation enables digital co-workers to translate machine language, which is difficult to compute, into language that people can easily understand.
NLP	Natural Language Processing	Natural language processing refers to computers learning to mimic human verbal and written language, used to enable chatbots and virtual agents to engage in human conversation.
	Neural Network	A computer architecture that behaves in a similar way to neural pathways in the human brain, where connections are made between computers and data, allowing the system to learn and improve through trial and error.
	North Star	A clear and compelling vision or goal that guides an organization's strategic direction.
OCR	Optical Character Recognition	Technology that enables written or typed data to be turned into digital text. OCR can be used to read, understand, and digitize information.
	Orchestration	Orchestration means automating your automations by using data and algorithms to gain an understanding of when the best time would be to perform tasks.

(continued)

Acronym	Term	Description
OCM	Organizational Change Management	The holistic approach to managing organizational transitions, including assessing the current state, identifying resistance points, and devising strategies to promote acceptance and engagement.
OD	Organizational Design	The process of aligning the shape and structure of an organization with its strategy to achieve its goals effectively.
	Organizational Design Models	Frameworks and methodologies used to assess internal and external factors, align organizational components, and facilitate effective decision making in the context of automation-first strategies.
	Organizational Structures	Different configurations of organizational hierarchies, such as hierarchical, flat, specialist networks, matrix, network-based, self-managing teams, and cooperative ownership structures, are tailored to support initiatives and future-of-work trends.
	Outcome-Driven Automation	Outcome-driven automation focuses on achieving specific business outcomes rather than automating tasks in isolation.
	Predictive Analytics	The practice of extracting insights from historical data to predict future outcomes and trends, enabling organizations to make informed decisions and take proactive actions.
	Process Improvement	Incremental changes made to existing processes to enhance efficiency and effectiveness, typically involving tweaking and iterating rather than a complete overhaul.
	Process Mining	Process mining involves extracting knowledge from event logs recorded by a system to enable organizations to discover, monitor, and improve their processes by identifying patterns, deviations, and bottlenecks.
	Process Re-engineering	A strategic approach to redesigning business processes from the ground up to achieve significant improvements in efficiency, effectiveness, and customer satisfaction.
	Quantum Computing	Faster computing power that results from not using traditional bits, which represent either 0 or 1, and instead using quantum bits or qubits, which can represent both 0 and 1 simultaneously. (I don't know what that means either, let's just say fast computers shall we?)

(continued)

Acronym	Term	Description
	Recruitment and Career Planning	Strategically sourcing both internal and external talent to build skilled automation teams and ensuring career development aligns with organizational goals.
	Remote Work	The practice of working outside of a traditional office environment, enabled by technology that allows employees to communicate and collaborate effectively from anywhere with an internet connection.
	Retinal Projection	A display technology that projects images directly onto the retina, creating a high-resolution, personalized visual experience without the need for screens or glasses.
ROI	Return on Investment	ROI measures the financial gains or cost savings generated by systems or by automation initiatives compared to the investment made in implementation.
	Risk Appetite	Risk appetite is how much uncertainty an organization can handle for success.
	Risk Tolerance	Risk tolerance is the level of risk an organization is comfortable to assume, within its limits.
	Risk Mitigation	Risk mitigation is about reducing or eliminating potential risks. It includes identifying risks, assessing their impact, prioritizing them, and implementing measures to manage them.
	Roadmap	A comprehensive timeline outlining the journey from the current state to the future state, including strategic milestones, success criteria, and the contributions of each business function.
RPA	Robotic Process Automation	Software that enables digital co-workers to carry out tasks or business processes within your existing systems and applications, following the step-by-step process that a human worker would normally do.
	Role Mapping	Redesigning current and future roles within the organization, ensuring alignment with goals and identifying necessary skills.
	Root Cause Analysis	Investigating the underlying causes of problems or inefficiencies in business processes, enabling targeted solutions and improvements to address the root causes rather than just symptoms.
	Skills Development	Investing in reskilling and upskilling initiatives to equip employees with the necessary competencies for an automation-driven future and a continuous learning and development culture.

(continued)

Acronym	Term	Description
SMART	SMART Objectives	A framework for setting objectives that are specific, measurable, achievable, relevant, and time-bound, ensuring clarity and effectiveness in goal-setting.
	Stakeholders	Stakeholders are individuals, groups, or entities that have an interest or stake in the outcomes of a project or initiative.
	Structured Data	Structured data are displayed in a predefined and expected format, whereas unstructured data have no typical definition such as text or audio.
	Succession Planning	Identifying and nurturing talent within the organization to fill critical roles, ensuring smooth transitions and long-term strategy realization.
	Talent Mapping	Matching skills and aspirations of employees with organizational needs to develop tailored career paths and succession plans.
	Talent Retention	Creating a supportive workplace with incentives, growth opportunities, and transparent communication to retain valuable employees and engender loyalty.
	Tech Stack	The selection and installation of technologies aligned with organizational goals and requirements.
TCO	Total Cost of Ownership	TCO reflects the total cost of owning and operating a product, system, or service over its entire life cycle, including initial investment and ongoing costs.
	Value Stream Mapping	Visualizing the end-to-end flow of value within a business process, identifying waste, delays, and opportunities for streamlining and improvement.
	What-If Analysis	Simulation and what-if analysis allow organizations to test different scenarios and predict outcomes before making changes. This helps in making informed decisions and minimizing risks.
WIIFM	What's In It For Me?	An engagement technique to describe the benefits for an individual so they can assess how a situation or proposal directly benefits them personally.
	Workflow	A defined sequence of steps that represent the systematic flow of work within an organization between departments, people, or systems, outlining the tasks, decisions, and interactions required.

Notes

Chapter 1

1. Lampron, "Why Saying Digital Transformation Is No Longer Right."
2. The Business Research Company, "Intelligent Automation Global Market Report 2024."

Chapter 2

1. Young, CIPD.
2. Gutterman, "Organizational Design."
3. Haden, Inc.com.
4. Bryan, McKinsey Quarterly.
5. Galbraith, Galbraith Management Consultants.
6. Abbas, Change Management Institute.
7. CIPD, "Organisation Design Factsheet."
8. Weisbord, "Organizational Diagnosis: Six Places to Look for Trouble With or Without a Theory.'
9. Minnaar, Corporate Rebels.

Chapter 3

1. Reddy, IndiaAI.
2. Scholnick, "The Evolution of Digital Transformation."

Chapter 4

1. Toyama, Public Affairs Publishing.
2. Tech UK, "Tech for Good."

Chapter 7

1. Pesce, (2023), *Getting Started With ChatGPT and AI Chatbots*.
2. Fehrend, Leapworks.
3. Amar, McKinsey.
4. Velimirovic, PhoenixNAP.
5. UIPath, Hyperautomation Fuels Growth for Heineken.
6. Allen, CloudPro.
7. Burnett, *The Autonomous Enterprise: Powered by AI*.
8. SS&C Blue Prism, "The Resounding Success of Equinix's Transformation Journey."

Chapter 8

1. Mather, *Super User Networks for Software Projects*.
2. Westberg, Quartr.

Chapter 9

1. Pink, *Drive: The Surprising Truth About What Motivates Us*.
2. Bapat, "Why You Should Let Employees Personalize Their Job Descriptions."
3. Prakash, Fortune.com.
4. Broom, World Economic Forum.
5. Star, SS&C Blue Prism.
6. Agile Manifestio Authors.
7. Cook, EY.com.
8. Aykens, Lowmaster, McRae, and Shepp, "9 Trends That Will Shape Work in 2024 and Beyond."
9. Wright, Retail Gazette.

Chapter 10

1. Mather, *Super User Networks for Software Projects*.
2. Ibid.
3. Ibid.

Chapter 11

1. Frauenheim, Great Place to Work.
2. Great Place to Work Company Profile, (2023).
3. Untitled Leader, "The Brave Leadership Lessons of Reshma Saujani."
4. Ian, Press Farm.
5. Raval, Financial Times.
6. Parsons, Apollo Advisors.

Chapter 12

1. Giles, New Scientist.
2. Iansiti and Lakhani, "Competing in the Age of AI."
3. Bort, Business Insider.
4. Halamka, Mayo Clinic Platform.

Chapter 13

1. United Nations Trade & Development, "Risk Culture and Risk Appetite."
2. Harrington, Voehl, and Voehl, Project Management Institute.

Chapter 14

1. European Commission, "AI Act."
2. Firth-Butterfield, World Economic Forum.
3. Paul, "'Disastrous' Lack of Diversity in AI Industry Perpetuates Bias, Study Finds."
4. Veenendaal, SS&C Blue Prism.
5. Erickson, Oracle.
6. Eusanio, A, Salesforce.
7. Unkefer, Accenture.
8. Dixon, Virtual Vocations.
9. Sivadasan, "Don't Go Backwards: Intelligent Automation and the New Hybrid Work Environment."
10. Yates, BuiltIn.

11. Chainey, World Economic Forum.
12. Manyika and Sneader, McKinsey.
13. Haluza, and Jungwirth, "Artificial Intelligence and Ten Societal Megatrends: An Exploratory Study Using GPT-3."
14. Gries and Naude, IZA Institute of Labor Economics.
15. Anderson and Raine, Pew Research Center.
16. Eisen, Galliher, Katz, and Turner Lee, Brookings.
17. Singer, "New A.I. Chatbot Tutors Could Upend Student Learning."
18. Kopp, World Economic Forum.
19. Bhatt and Muduli, "Artificial Intelligence in Learning and Development: A Systematic Literature Review."
20. Anderson and Smith, Pew Research Center.
21. Anderson and Raine, Pew Research Center.
22. Shine, World Economic Forum.
23. Anderson and Raine, Pew Research Center.
24. Chakraborty, Tech UK.
25. Daugherty and Wilson, "Collaborative Intelligence: Humans and AI Are Joining Forces."
26. Anderson and Smith, Pew Research Center.
27. Broom, World Economic Forum.
28. Cacoveanu, Yarooms.
29. Roboyo, "Intelligent Automation in a Post-Pandemic World."
30. Feijoo and Kwon, "Harnessing Artificial Intelligence (AI) to Increase Wellbeing for All."
31. Haluza and Jungwirth, "Artificial Intelligence and Ten Societal Megatrends: An Exploratory Study Using GPT-3."
32. Anderson and Raine, Pew Research Center.
33. Thee, Personal Communication to Mather.
34. Haluza and Jungwirth, "Artificial Intelligence and Ten Societal Megatrends: An Exploratory Study Using GPT-3."
35. Ibid.
36. Meacham, Learn, and Live, Associate for Talent Development.
37. Norman, AIMonks.io.
38. Anderson and Raine, Pew Research Center.
39. Gilfix, IBM.

40. Kelly, "AI Is Coming for Our Jobs! Could Universal Basic Income Be the Solution?"

41. Santens, Evonomics.

42. Ferdosi, Lewchuk, McDowell, and Ross, Unesco.

43. Kelly, "AI Is Coming for Our Jobs! Could Universal Basic Income Be the Solution?"

44. Anderson and Raine, Pew Research Center.

45. Harding, *AI Needs You: How We Can Change AI's Future and Save Our Own.*

References

Abbas, T. 2020. "Burke Litwin Model of Change." *Change Management Institute.* Accessed May 2024. https://changemanagementinsight.com/burke-litwin-model-of-change/.

Agile Manifesto Authors. 2001. *Agile Manifesto.* Accessed April 2024. https://agilemanifesto.org/.

Ahuja, K and I. Bala. 2021, "Role of Artificial Intelligence and IoT in Next Generation Education System." *Intelligence of Things: AI-IoT Based Critical-Applications and Innovations.* Springer. Accessed April 2024. https://doi.org/10.1007/978-3-030-82800-4_8.

Allen, K. 2022. "Hyperautomation in Action: The Most Exciting Examples." *CloudPro.* www.itpro.com/business-strategy/automation/367382/hyperautomation-inaction-most-exciting-examples.

Amar, J. 2022. "Smart-Scheduling: How to Solve Workforce Planning Challenges with AI." *McKinsey.* Accessed May 2024. www.mckinsey.com/capabilities/operations/our-insights/smart-scheduling-how-to-solve-workforce-planning-challenges-with-ai.

Anderson, J. and A. Smith. 2014. "AI, Robotics, and the Future of Jobs." *Pew Research Center.* Accessed May 2024. www.pewresearch.org/internet/2014/08/06/future-of-jobs/.

Anderson, J. and L. Raine. 2018. "Artificial Intelligence and the Future of Humans." *Pew Research Center.* Accessed May 2024. www.pewresearch.org/internet/2018/12/10/artificial-intelligence-and-the-future-of-humans.

Anderson, J. and L. Raine. 2018. "Solutions to Address AI's Anticipated Negative Impacts." *Pew Research Center.* Accessed May 2024. Anshuman, A. 2023. "Leadership In The Age Of AI: Leveraging Intelligent Automation." *Forbes.* Accessed April 2024. www.forbes.com/sites/forbesbusinesscouncil/2023/08/23/leadership-in-the-age-of-ai-leveraging-intelligent-automation/.

Aykens, P., K. Lowmaster, E. McRae, and J. Shepp. 2024. "9 Trends That Will Shape Work in 2024 and Beyond." *Harvard Business Review.* Accessed April 2024. https://hbr.org/2024/01/9-trends-that-will-shape-work-in-2024-and-beyond.

Bachmann, H., R. Ligon, and D. Skerritt. 2022. "The Powerful Role Financial Incentives Can Play in a Transformation." *McKinsey.* Accessed April 2024. www.mckinsey.com/capabilities/transformation/our-insights/the-powerful-role-financial-incentives-can-play-in-a-transformation.

Bapat, V. 2018. "Why You Should Let Employees Personalize Their Job Descriptions." *Harvard Business Review*. Accessed April 2024.

Barkin, I., P. Bornet, and J. Wirtz. 2021 *Intelligent Automation: Welcome to the World of Hyperautomation - Learn How to Harness Artificial Intelligence to Boost Business & Make Our World More Human*. World Scientific.

Benzell, S and Y.V. Yifan. 2021. "Simulating the Future of Global Automation, its Consequences, and Evaluating Policy Options." *VoxEU*, Accessed April 2024. https://cepr.org/voxeu/columns/simulating-future-global-automation-its-consequences-and-evaluating-policy-options.

Bhatt, P. and A.Muduli. 2023. "Artificial Intelligence in Learning and Development: A Systematic Literature Review." *European Journal of Training and Development* 47. Accessed April 2024. https://doi.org/10.1108/EJTD-09-2021-0143.

Bollard, A., E. Larrea, A. Singla, and R. Sood. (2017), 'The Next-Generation Operating Model for the Digital World." *McKinsey*. Accessed April 2024. www.mckinsey.com/capabilities/mckinsey-digital/our-insights/the-next-generation-operating-model-for-the-digital-world.

Bort, J. 2017. "How Salesforce CEO Marc Benioff Uses Artificial Intelligence to End Internal Politics at Meetings." *Business Insider*. Accessed June 2024. www.businessinsider.com/benioff-uses-ai-to-end-politics-at-staff-meetings-2017-5.

Briggs, J and D. Kodnani. 2023. "Generative AI could raise global GDP by 7%." *Goldman Sachs*. Accessed April 2024. www.goldmansachs.com/intelligence/pages/generative-ai-could-raise-global-gdp-by-7-percent.html.

Broom, D. 2023. "Four-Day Work Week Trial in Spain Leads to Healthier Workers, Less Pollution', *World Economic Forum*. Accessed February 2024. www.weforum.org/agenda/2023/10/surprising-benefits-four-day-week/.

Bryan, L. 2008. "Enduring Ideas: The7--S Framework." *McKinsey Quarterly*. Accessed May 2024. www.mckinsey.com/capabilities/strategy-and-corporate-finance/our-insights/enduring-ideas-the-7-s-framework.

Burnett, S. 2022. *The Autonomous Enterprise: Powered by AI*. British Computer Society.

Cacoveanu, A. 2023. "The Promise of AI in Elevating Employee Experience." *Yarooms*. Accessed January 2024. www.yarooms.com/blog/the-promise-of-ai-in-elevating-employee-experience.

Campbell, P. 2023 "Using Intelligent Automation to Rethink the Art of the Possible and Improve Citizen Experience." *Capita*. Accessed May 2024. www.capita.co.uk/our-thinking/using-intelligent-automation-rethink-art-possible-and-improve-citizen-experience

Case IQ. "Employee Relations Best Practices: Costco's Approach to HR." *Case IQ*. www.caseiq.com/resources/employee-relations-best-practices-costco/.

Chainey, R. 2017. "The Global Economy will be $16 Trillion Bigger by 2030 Thanks to AI." *World Economic Forum.* Accessed May 2024.

Chakraborty, S. 2024. "AI and Society: A Case Study on Positive Social Change." *Tech UK,* Accessed May 2024. www.techuk.org/resource/ai-and-society-a-case-study-on-positive-social-change.html.

CIPD. 2023. "Organisation Design." *CIPD.* Accessed May 2024. www.cipd.org/uk/knowledge/factsheets/organisational-development-design-factsheet/.

Cook, M. 2021. "Why The Future of Work Will Depend on the Future of Total Reward." *EY.com.* Accessed April 2024. www.ey.com/en_hr/workforce/why-the-future-of-work-will-depend-on-the-future-of-total-reward.

Daugherty, P and H.J. Wilson. 2018. "Collaborative Intelligence: Humans and AI Are Joining Forces." *Harvard Business Review.* Accessed May 2024. https://hbr.org/2018/07/collaborative-intelligence-humans-and-ai-are-joining-forces.

Davenport, T and J. Foutty. 2018. "AI-Driven Leadership." *MIT Sloan.* Accessed August 2024. https://sloanreview.mit.edu/article/ai-driven-leadership/.

Dignan, L. 2023. "What is a Process Digital Twin? The Answer is Evolving Due to Process Mining." *Celonis.* Accessed April 2024. www.celonis.com/blog/what-is-a-digital-twin-the-answer-is-evolving-due-to-process-mining/.

Dixon, B. 2024. "AI and Remote Work: Exploring How Artificial Intelligence Could Transform Telecommuting." *Virtual Vocations.* Accessed May 2024.

Eisen, N., C. Galliher, J. Katz. L.N. Turner. 2023. "AI Can Strengthen U.S. Democracy—and Weaken It." *Brookings.* Accessed April 2024. www.brookings.edu/articles/ai-can-strengthen-u-s-democracy-and-weaken-it/.

Erickson, J. 2023. "What Is Intelligent Automation?." *Oracle.* Accessed April 2024. www.oracle.com/uk/cloud/intelligent-automation/#ia-benefits.

European Commission. 2024. "AI Act." Accessed April 2024. https://digital-strategy.ec.europa.eu/en/policies/regulatory-framework-ai.

Eusanio, A. 2019. "35 Inspiring Quotes About AI." *Salesforce.* Accessed April 2024. www.salesforce.com/eu/blog/ai-quotes/.

Fehrend, K. 2024. "Reusability in Test Automation and RPA." *Leapworks.* Accessed May 2024. www.leapwork.com/learn/reusable-sub-flows.

Feijoo, C. and Y. Kwon. 2020. "Harnessing Artificial Intelligence (AI) to Increase Wellbeing for All: The Case for a New Technology Diplomacy." *Science Direct TeleCommunications Policy* 44(6), Accessed February 2024. www.sciencedirect.com/science/article/pii/S030859612030080X#sec1.

Ferdosi, M., W. Lewchuk, T. McDowell and S. Ross, S. 2022. "On How Ontario Trialed Basic Income." *Unesco.* Accessed April 2024. https://en.unesco.org/inclusivepolicylab/analytics/how-ontario-trialed-basic-income.

Firth-Butterfield, K. 2021. "5 Ways to Get More Women Working in AI." *World Economic Forum.* Accessed April 2024. www.weforum.org/agenda/2021/08/5-ways-increase-women-working-ai/.

Frauenheim, E. 2020. "How Cisco Has Blended Bold Action With Humble Leadership." *Great Place to Work.* Accessed June 2024. www.greatplacetowork. com/resources/blog/how-cisco-has-blended-bold-action-with-humble-leadership.

Galbraith, J. "Star Model™." *Galbraith Management Consultants.* Accessed May 2024. https://jaygalbraith.com/services/star-model/.

Georgieva, K. 2024. "AI Will Transform the Global Economy. Let's Make Sure It Benefits Humanity." *IMF.* Accessed February 2024. www.imf.org/en/Blogs/Articles/2024/01/14/ai-will-transform-the-global-economy-lets-make-sure-it-benefits-humanity.

Giles, J. 2012. "Watson Turns Medic: Supercomputer to Diagnose Disease." *New Scientist.* Accessed June 2024. www.newscientist.com/article/mg21528796-400-watson-turns-medic-supercomputer-to-diagnose-disease.

Gilfix, M. 2021. "Intelligent Automation Uses Advanced AI to Give Humans the Gift of Time." *IBM.* Accessed August 2024. www.ibm.com/blog/intelligent-automation-uses-advanced-ai-to-give-humans-the-gift-of-time/.

Golombek, M. 2022. "Hyperautomation: 8 Steps to Turn Theory Into Action." *Exasol.* Accessed April 2024. www.exasol.com/resource/insights-8-steps-to-put-hyperautomation-into-practice/.

Great Place to Work Company Profile. 2023. "Great Place to Work." Accessed June 2024. www.greatplacetowork.com/certified-company/1000064.

Gries, T. and W Naude. 2018. "Artificial Intelligence, Jobs, Inequality and Productivity: Does Aggregate Demand Matter?" *IZA Institute of Labor Economics.* Accessed April 2024. https://docs.iza.org/dp12005.pdf.

Gutterman, A. 2023. "Organizational Design." *SSRN.* Accessed April 2024. http://dx.doi.org/10.2139/ssrn.4541482.

Haden, J. 2018. "Amazon Founder Jeff Bezos: This Is How Successful People Make Such Smart Decisions." *Inc.com.* Accessed May 2024. www.inc.com/jeff-haden/amazon-founder-jeff-bezos-this-is-how-successful-people-make-such-smart-decisions.html.

Halamka, M.D.J. 2022. "Can Digital Twins Improve Patient Care?" *Mayo Clinic Platform.* Accessed June 2024. www.mayoclinicplatform.org/2022/07/12/can-digital-twins-improve-patient-care/.

Haluza, D and D. Jungwirth. 2023. "Artificial Intelligence and Ten Societal Megatrends: An Exploratory Study Using GPT-3." *Systems* 11(3). Accessed April 2024. https://doi.org/10.3390/systems11030120.

Harding, V. 2024. *AI Needs You: How We Can Save AI's Future and Save Our Own.* Princeton University Press.

Harrington, H. J., F. Voehl, and C.F. Voehl. 2015. "Model for Sustainable Change." *Project Management Institute White Paper*.

Hindle, J., J. Smith. M. Stanton, and L. Willcocks. 2024. *Maximizing Value with Automation and Digital Transformation: A Realist's Guide*. Spinger Link Publishing.

Hindle, J., MC. Lacity, and L. Willcocks. 2019. *Becoming Strategic With Robotic Process Automation*. SB Publishing.

How, N. 2018. *Run Fast: The Definitive Guide to Accelerating Technology Projects*. Rethink Press.

Ian. 2024. "Susan Wojcickis Leadership Style: What Makes her Successful." *Press Farm*. Accessed June 2024. https://press.farm/susan-wojcickis-leadership-style-and-success/.

Iansiti, M and K. Lakhani. 2020. "Competing in the Age of AI." *Harvard Business Review*. Accessed June 2024. https://hbr.org/2020/01/competing-in-the-age-of-ai.

Jones, A. S. Bull and G. Castellano. 2018. "I Know That Now, I'm Going to Learn This Next" Promoting Self-regulated Learning with a Robotic Tutor." *International Journal of Social Robotics* 10. Accessed February 2024. Available at https://doi.org/10.1007/s12369-017-0430-y.

Karwal, D. 2020 "The Automated Enterprise: Digital Reinvention Through Intelligent Automation." *Independent*.

Kelly, P. 2023. "AI is Coming for Our Jobs! Could Universal Basic Income be the Solution?', *The Guardian*. Accessed April 2024. www.theguardian.com/global-development/2023/nov/16/ai-is-coming-for-our-jobs-could-universal-basic-income-be-the-solution.

King, D., R. Sidhu, D. Skelsey, R. Smith. 2015. *The Effective Change Manager's Handbook*. Kogan Page Ltd.

Kopp, W. 2023. "How AI Can Accelerate Students' Holistic Development and Make Teaching more Fulfilling." *World Economic Forum*. Accessed June 2024. www.weforum.org/agenda/2023/05/ai-accelerate-students-holistic-development-teaching-fulfilling/.

Lampron, D. 2023. "Why Saying Digital Transformation Is No Longer Right." *Techopedia*. Accessed April 2024. www.techopedia.com/why-saying-digital-transformation-is-no-longer-right/.

Leifer, L.; M. Lewrick and P. Link. 2018. *The Design Thinking Playbook: Mindful Digital Transformation of Teams, Products, Services, Businesses and Ecosystems*. Wiley.

Manyika, J and K. Sneader. 2019. "AI, Automation and the Future of Work." *McKinsey*. Accessed April 2024. www.mckinsey.com/featured-insights/future-of-work/ai-automation-and-the-future-of-work-ten-things-to-solve-for.

Mather, J. 2023. *Super User Networks for Software Projects: Best Practices in Training and Change Management.* British Computer Society.

Meacham, M. 2020. *AI in Talent Development: Capitalize on the AI Revolution to Transform the Way You Work, Learn, and Live, Associate for Talent Development.*

Meissner, P. 2021. "Artificial Intelligence will Transform Decision-Making. Here's how." *World Economic Forum,* Accessed March 2024 www.weforum. org/agenda/2023/09/how-artificial-intelligence-will-transform-decision-making/.

Minaar, J. 2023. "Talent Mapping: How HR Can Use a Skills-Focused Approach." *Corporate Rebels.* Accessed July 2024. www.corporate-rebels.com/ blog/musks-algorithm-to-cut-bureaucracy.

Minnaar, J. 2019. "Make Work Fun." *Corporate Rebels.*

Norman, S. 2023. "AI in Language Translation: Bridging Global Divides." *Medium.* Accessed August 2024. https://medium.com/aimonks/ai-in-language-translation-bridging-global-divides-69409856e136.

Paige, M. 2023. "The Evolution Of Digital Transformation: From Pre-Internet To Post-Pandemic." *Hatchworks.* Accessed June 2024. https://hatchworks. com/blog/product-design/history-digital-transformation/.

Parsons, M. 2023. "The Unconventional Leadership of Jensen Huang: Inside Nvidia's Unique Organizational Culture." *Apollo Advisors.* Accessed June 2024. www.apolloadvisor.com/unconventional-leadership-of-jensen-huang-inside-nvidias-unique-organizational-culture/.

Paul, K. 2019. "'Disastrous' Lack of Diversity in AI Industry Perpetuates Bias, Study Finds." *Guardian.* Accessed December 2023.

Pesce, M. 2023. "Getting Started with ChatGPT and AI Chatbots: An introduction to generative AI tools." *British Computer Society.*

Pink, D. 2011. *Drive: The Surprising Truth About What Motivates Us.* Canongate Books.

Prakash, P. 2023. "AI Should Make the 4-Day Work Week Possible for Millions of Workers." *Fortune.com.* Accessed February 2024. https://fortune.com/ europe/2023/11/24/4-four-day-workweek-u-k-employeesai-tools-chatgpt/.

Raval, A. 2023. "Ginni Rometty: Leadership, Legacy and a New Mission." *Financial Times.* Accessed June 2024. www.ft.com/content/beae436b-ce83-43ab-9254-70f9f3b6b1b3.

Reddy, V. 2023. "The Evolution of Generative AI: Capabilities, Future and Implications for Clinical Research." *IndiaAI.* Accessed August 2024. https:// indiaai.gov.in/article/the-evolution-of-generative-ai-capabilities-future-and-implications-for-clinical-research.

Roboyo. 2022. "Intelligent Automation in a Post-Pandemic World." *Roboyo.* Accessed May 2024. https://roboyo.global/blog/intelligent-automation-in-a-post-pandemic-world/.

Santens, S. 2012. "Universal Basic Income Accelerates Innovation by Reducing Our Fear of Failure." *Evonomics*. Accessed April 2024. https://evonomics. com/universal-basic-income-accelerates-innovation-reducing-fear-failure/.

Scholnick, I. 2021. "The Evolution of Digital Transformation." *Forbes*. Accessed April 2024. www.forbes.com/sites/forbestechcouncil/2021/08/12/the-evolution-of-digital-transformation/?sh=3461be1e6fb8.

Shine, I. 2023. "These are the Jobs Most Likely to be Lost – and Created – Because of AI." *World Economic Forum*. Accessed July 2024. www.weforum. org/agenda/2023/05/jobs-lost-created-ai-gpt/.

Singer, N. 2023. "New A.I. Chatbot Tutors Could Upend Student Learning." *New York Times*. Accessed April 2024. www.nytimes. com/2023/06/08/business/khan-ai-gpt-tutoring-bot.html; www.blue-prism.com/resources/blog/the-future-of-work/.

Sivadasan, B. 2021. "Don't Go Backwards: Intelligent Automation And The New Hybrid Work Environment." *Forbes*. Accessed May 2024.

SS&C Blue Prism. n.d. "The Resounding Success of Equinix's Transformation Journey." Accessed May 2024. www.blueprism.com/resources/case-studies/the-resounding-success-of-equinixs-transformation-journey/.

Stanford, N. 2018. *Organization Design: The Practitioner's Guide*. Routledge.

Star, K. 2022. "Human-Centered Automation and The Future of Work." *SS&C Blue Prism*. Accessed May 2024.

Starita, L. 2021. "Would You Let Artificial Intelligence Make Your Pay Decisions?" *Gartner*. Accessed April 2024. www.gartner.com/smarterwithgartner/would-you-let-artificial-intelligence-make-your-pay-decisions.

Tech UK. n.d. "Tech for Good." Accessed July 2024. www.techuk.org/who-we-are/tech-for-good.html.

The Business Research Company. 2024. "Intelligent Automation Global Market Report 2024." *The Business Research Company*, Accessed February 2024. www. thebusinessresearchcompany.com/report/intelligent-process-automation-global-market-report. Thee, Lisa, (2024), Personal communication to Mather, Jayne

Theuerkauf, J. 2019. "How to Get Your Organization In The Right Mindset For Automation." *Forbes*. Accessed February 2024. www.forbes.com/sites/forbesbusinessdevelopmentcouncil/2019/12/04/how-to-get-your-organization-in-the-right-mindset-for-automation/.

Timms, M.J. 2016. "Letting Artificial Intelligence in Education Out of the Box: Educational Cobots and Smart Classrooms." *International Journal of Artificial Intelligence in Education*. Accessed February 2024. https://doi.org/10.1007/s40593-016-0095-y.

Toyama, K. 2015. *Geek Heresy: Rescuing Social Change from the Cult of Technology*. Public Affairs Publishing.

UIPath. n.d. "Hyperautomation Fuels Growth for Heineken | UiPath." Accessed March 2024. www.uipath.com/resources/automation-case-studies/hyperautomation-fuels-growth-for-heineken.

United Nations Trade & Development. n.d. "Risk Culture and Risk Appetite." Accessed January 2024. https://resilientmaritimelogistics.unctad.org/guidebook/2-risk-culture-and-appetite.

Unkefer, H. 2017. "Accenture Report: Artificial Intelligence Has Potential to Increase Corporate Profitability in 16 Industries by an Average of 38 Percent by 2035." *Accenture*. Accessed December 2023.

Untitled Leader. "The Brave Leadership Lessons of Reshma Saujani." Accessed June 2024. www.untitledleader.com/lessons-in-leadership/the-brave-leadership-lessons-of-reshma-saujani/.

Veenendaal, A. 2024. "Responsible AI: 5 Principles for Implementation"SS&C Blue Prism. Accessed May 2024. www.blueprism.com/resources/blog/responsible-ai/.

Velimirovic, A. 2021. "Automation vs Orchestration: Overlapping but Different IT Concepts." *PhoenixNAP*. Accessed May 2024. https://phoenixnap.com/blog/orchestration-vs-automation.

Watson, R. 2021. "How to Tackle Any Challenging Change Risks With Change Impact Analysis." *Stracl*. Accessed February 2024. https://stracl.com/blog/how-to-tackle-change-risks-withchange-impact-analysis.

Weisbord, M.R. 1976. "Organizational Diagnosis: Six Places to Look for Trouble with or without a Theory." *Sage Journals, Group & Organization Studies*1(4).

West, D.M. 2018. "The Future of Work: Robots, AI, and Automation." *Brookings Institution*

Westberg, P. 2024. "Inside Netflix: Innovation, Originals, and Cultural Phenomena." *Quartr*. Accessed April 2024. https://quartr.com/insights/company-research/inside-netflix-innovation-originals-and-cultural-phenomena.

Westover, J. 2022. "Adaptive Organizational And Work Design For The Future Of Work." *Forbes*. Accessed December 2023. www.forbes.com/sites/forbescoachescouncil/2022/09/30/adaptive-organizational-and-work-design-for-the-future-of-work/?sh=71ed64ac6f58.

Willcocks, L. 2021. *Global Business: Strategy in Context*.SB Publishing

Wright, G. 2022. "Timpson CEO Offers Up Free Holiday Homes for Staff." *Retail Gazette*. Accessed March 2024. ww.weforum.org/agenda/2017/06/the-global-economy-will-be-14-bigger-in-2030-because-of-ai/.

Yates, C. 2022 "Intelligent Automation Can Help Startups Scale Faster." *BuiltIn*. Accessed May 2024. https://builtin.com/founders-entrepreneurship/intelligent-automation-can-help-startups-scale-faster.

About the Author

Jayne Mather is a distinguished expert in software implementation and brings decades of experience in leading processes, training, and change management on technology projects. She spends her time consulting on all things change and transformation for some of the biggest brands on the planet. Her impressive credentials—CIPD, MBA, and certifications in agile project management, change management, and intelligent automation—equip her to lead organizations through their digital transformation journey effectively. Passionate about her subject matter, when she's not writing about the future of work, she's reading or talking about it.

Jayne is also the author of *Super User Networks for Software Projects: Best Practices for Training and Change Management*, praised as an "indispensable companion for anyone seeking hands-on expertise in driving successful transformations." Find out more at www.jaynemather.com.

Index

www.ingramcontent.com/pod-product-compliance
Ingram Content Group UK Ltd.
Pitfield, Milton Keynes, MK11 3LW, UK
UKHW021852250325
456717UK00006B/80